PROSPECTING THROUGH POSITIONING

How To Continually Fill Your Pipeline With Highly- Qualified, Highly-Motivated Prospects Without Ever Having To Cold Call Again

Chris Carlson

PROSPECTING THROUGH POSITIONING

By Chris Carlson

Copyright 2016

ISBN-13: 978-1530609703
ISBN-10: 1530609704

About The Author

Before becoming a sales and marketing consultant, Chris Carlson spent 20 years in the insurance industry as a Salesperson, Sales Manager and National Sales Director. Since 2003, Chris has worked with clients from large corporations to small business owners, helping them to grow sales, increase profits and create systems that will continually attract ideal clients.

In his consulting practice, Chris works with companies to insure they are focused on the most important step in the sales process, effectively targeting the right types of clients. By identifying The Ideal Client, companies can now create a Marketing Playbook that leverages the *Prospecting Through Positioning* methods, creating a transformation in client acquisition.

Table of Contents

INTRODUCTION

During my 30+ years in sales, I have always thought that selling was easy, but prospecting was a bitch. Once in front of a prospect, it has always been easy for me to first, qualify the prospect. They might be somebody who immediately needs what I offer, they might be somebody who eventually will need what I offer or they just might not be a prospect at all. Once I determine this, I can move them through my sales system and either they will be come a client or not. Again, selling is the easy part, getting in front of them can be challenging. And, without an effective prospecting strategy, it is even more challenging.

It comes to no one's surprise that selling has changed dramatically over the last 20 years. When I started my sales career in the early 1980's, the two main options for me in terms of prospecting were calling the prospect on the phone or stopping by their office. Sure, some companies did direct mail and some might have had budgets that allowed them to advertise in newspapers or on radio or television, but most of us only had the phone and shoe leather to prospect for new opportunities. While it might be hard for you to believe this, but when I started my sales career, there were no cell phones, no fax machines (funny how fax machines have literally come and gone in my selling lifetime), no voice mail, no Internet, no e-mail, no texting, no Facebook and no social media. It certainly was a different landscape back then.

The introduction of the Internet and the incredible advances in technology have created both opportunities and challenges for salespeople. It is becoming increasingly challenging to have an actual conversation with a prospect. Sure, you can "like" somebody on

Facebook or "connect" with them on LinkedIn, but getting an actual meeting with a person can be incredibly frustrating. After all, almost nobody answers their phone and most prospects will delete your voice mail message within 3 seconds if they don't know who you are. In a post 9/11 world, many buildings have established security barriers that prevent you from entering the building to "roam the floors" to make unsolicited cold calls. While many salespeople are stuck in the past, the smart salespeople have adapted to the changes and are positioning themselves as the experts in their niche.

With all the changes, how then do salespeople effectively and efficiently prospect for new opportunities? As you think of both the opportunities and challenges in this new prospecting world, I want to issue you this challenge. Instead of you chasing down prospects, why not have them come to you? How would your business or practice look if you had prospects who are both qualified and motivated and are asking you for the help your product or service can provide? Fantasy? I think not.

To have prospects lining up to do business with you, you *do* have to do things differently. And remarkably, the things you need to do are pretty simple. Simple yes, easy no. Most readers of this book will not act upon the ideas that I will discuss or the suggestions that I will make. While that is certainly your prerogative, you will be missing out on the most exciting and prosperous prospecting activities that exist today. You can remain firmly in the past, in which you continue to do unproductive prospecting activities, hoping that miracle will occur, **OR**, you can take advantage of all the opportunities that the Sales Gods have laid out before you.

I hope you keep an open mind as we explore the concept of Prospecting Through Positioning.

2

PART 1

TWO IMPORTANT LINES

Two Important Lines

There are two important "lines" that we need to talk about when it comes to Prospecting. The first is the Line of Credibility and the second is The Buy Line. Once you embrace these two lines, prospecting becomes so much easier. Ignore them and you will experience continual frustration and lack of results.

The Line of Credibility

According to various reports, it is estimated that each of us is bombarded by over 1500 marketing messages per day (some reports claim the number is over 3000 a day). This might seem like a huge number to you, but think of all the messages that come at you from sources like:

> ➢ E-mail
> ➢ Newspaper
> ➢ Radio
> ➢ T.V.
> ➢ Internet
> ➢ LinkedIn
> ➢ Facebook
> ➢ Instagram
> ➢ Billboards
> ➢ Signage on Trucks
> ➢ Signage on Buildings

So when you think about it, your brain is overwhelmed by these daily marketing messages. And what does your brain almost instantly do when it receives one of these marketing messages? That's right, it ignores them. Your challenge as a salesperson is that your marketing (prospecting) messages are lumped into the thousands of messages and are most likely ignored like the rest. So, your biggest challenge is to get your prospects to pay attention to you.

Now, all is not lost. After all, there are many of these thousands of marketing messages that you DO pay attention to. On a consistent basis, the ones you pay attention to are from a credible source that you know, like and/or trust. Maybe it is a source that has helped you in the past. Maybe it is a source that was referred to you by a friend. Maybe it is a source that you read about and are intrigued to learn more. In order for your prospects to pay attention to your message, you must establish credibility so they want more from you. In other words, you have to come in above The Line of Credibility. When you come in above The Line of Credibility, you do not get stuck in the "noise" with all the other messages. Instead, you stand out above the crowd and your messages get through, get digested and often get acted upon.

I was first exposed to the concept of The Line of Credibility when I listened to a presentation given by Peter Diamondis, best known for being the founder and chairman of the X Prize Foundation and the co-founder and executive chairman of Singularity University. Diamondis was talking about this Line of Credibility in a much broader sense, but it immediately hit me that this is exactly what salespeople face in their on-going prospecting efforts.

The genesis of this book is to discuss the three ways to come in above The Line of Credibility. They are, Publishing, Speaking and Referrals. If you focus your attention on these three activities, you will have all the prospects you need coming into your sales pipeline. Ignore them and prospecting sucks!

Think for a moment about an initial meeting you had with a prospect in which you had massive amounts of credibility in the prospect's eyes before you showed up. That credibility could be because you were referred in, it could be because the prospect watched you give a presentation or maybe the prospect consumed information that you had written or recorded. Armed with this credibility, wasn't there a different vibe to meeting? From the moment you walked in, and then all the way through the meeting, wasn't the conversation so much easier and so much more robust? Chances are there was a clear, agreed upon next step in the process. You probably left the meeting on a high.

The question you have to ask yourself is, "why aren't all my meetings like this?" Keep reading and you will find out how to make sure all of your meetings with prospects can be this way.

The Buy Line

The best way to describe The Buy Line is using this graphic:

0 --100

The number 0 represents where your prospect is in terms of having no thoughts about your product or service. The number 100 represents when they are actually buying your product or service.

In sales, you are constantly asking yourself a question like, "I wonder when they are going to be ready to buy?" You obviously want most of your prospects to be close to 100, since that is when the cash register rings for you. But the reality is, at any given moment, very few of your potential prospects are near 100. The overwhelming majority are somewhere between 0 and 80 on The Buy Line.

Companies and salespeople make two critical mistakes in regards to The Buy Line.

The first mistake is that they spend all of their time, effort and money on prospects that are in the 80-90 range on The Buy Line. This happens because they either (1) force their way into the prospect's life and try to convince them to buy now or (2) the get invited in by the prospect to quote, present or propose because the prospect needs competitive bids to keep his/her incumbent provider honest. When this happens, all of your sirens go off and all hands are on deck to try and win the business. Everyone is excited about this great prospect. Unfortunately, far too often you do not get the business. But you do hear things like, "we really like what we saw."

"It was really close." "It was tough to not choose you." These kind words help heal our wounds, and tragically condition us to do the same thing the next time around.

The second mistake companies and salespeople make is that they forget to market to prospects all the way through The Buy Line. In order to establish a relationship, trust and credibility, it is imperative that you communicate, market and add value from 0 to 100. As stated before, the majority of your prospects are between 0 and 80 on The Buy Line. You must continually nurture these relationships so when they get into the 80-90 "hot range," you have already established your credibility and are the obvious solution.

Now in your world, you might have terms that relate to The Buy Line, like Suspect, Prospect, Qualified and Ready To Close. These are typically associated with opportunities that are in your actual pipeline. But keep this in mind, most of these opportunities are pretty far down The Buy Line. While it is good to have these opportunities, you cannot forget that the majority of your future prospects are not even in your sales pipeline and yet you must continue to develop and deepen a relationship with these people.

The Line of Credibility and The Buy Line are inherently woven together. If you have credibility and demonstrate, communicate and market that credibility throughout The Buy Line, you will almost by default, go to the front of the line when your prospect is ready to buy your product or service.

As you go through the rest of your selling career, always be mindful of these two lines and use this knowledge as an unfair advantage in your prospecting and marketing efforts.

CHRIS CARLSON

PART 2

PUBLISHING

Publishing

The first broad category we are going to discuss regarding Prospecting Through Positioning is Publishing. The concept of publishing in today's selling world is so much different than when I started in sales. Back then, it was both complicated and expensive to do any time of publishing. Additionally, some of the mediums we are going discuss were not even available back then.

With the advances in technology, publishing has never been easier or cheaper (in some cases the cost is zero). This technology has unleashed incredible creativity, resulting in tools and platforms that allow you to establish credibility and then promote this credibility to your prospects, clients and Centers of Influence. The publishing ideas we are going to discuss in this book include:

- Articles
- White Papers
- Blogs
- Newsletters
- E-Newsletters
- Videos
- Webinars
- Webcasts
- Virtual Summits
- Podcasting
- Writing A Book
- Writing An E-Book
- Direct Mail

As you go through this book, be thinking about which of these methodologies will work for you. You might decided to use just one of these methods or use multiple methods. I would challenge you to get outside your comfort zone when considering this. Chances are, the methods that you might be "scared" of, are the ones you should be doing.

Articles

For many, the thought of writing even a few pages is daunting. Yet, writing articles is probably the easiest and quickest way to launch yourself into this concept of publishing.

Articles are typically between 2 to 3 pages and are a tremendous way to add value to your target market. Here is a 4-step process for using articles in your prospecting efforts:

1. Determine the topic/content of the article
2. Write the article
3. Submit the article for publication
4. Promote your article

Determine The Topic/Content Of The Article

As you consider the topic and content of the article you are going to write, do not forget why you are writing the article. The article SHOULD be to add value to those you serve. The more value the article adds, the more credibility you will establish.

Always remember that you should look at the article through the lens of your ideal client. Remember their favorite radio station is WIIFM (What's In It For Me), so make them want to "hear" your message.

Write The Article

I have always felt that once you know the topic you want to write about, the writing becomes easy. But, you still have to sit down and write the article. My advice is to set aside one hour on your calendar, eliminate all other distractions and then just write for one hour. Don't try and be perfect, just let it flow. You can always revise and edit later. If you commit to doing this, you will have the framework of your article.

Here is an idea if you are someone who just hates writing. Have someone interview you on the topic you have chosen. Record the interview, have the recording transcribed (http://www.rev.com) and then edit. You can choose to have the article left in an interview format or you can just take the content you talked about and format into a traditional article.

Submit The Article For Publication

You probably have a pretty good idea of the publications that your ideal clients read. These are the publications to which you are going to submit your article. Be mindful that not all of your articles are going to be published, but you should make the effort. My experience is after you have submitted a couple of articles to a publication (and assuming they are good articles), then these publications will actually start to reach out to you.

If you believe writing articles is one of the methods you are going to focus on, you can even suggest to the publication that you would like to write a monthly article. It would not be unusual that you could be a regular columnist in the publication. You have to determine if this is right for you and if you have the capacity to produce an article as frequently as the publication is sent out.

Promote Your Article

Once your article is published, make sure you promote it everywhere, on your website, on LinkedIn, on Facebook, Twitter and any other place you have. Make sure you mention the article in your e-newsletter and/or printed newsletter.

Make sure you send a copy of the article to your clients and Centers of Influence. You could send it via e-mail, but I promise that it will have a bigger impact if you send a hard copy with a short hand-written note. When you schedule a meeting with a prospect, send them the article in advance of your meeting. This is going to give you credibility before you even meet them.

Even if your article is not published anywhere, you can still use it in your marketing efforts. Instead of saying "here is an article that was published in **The Business Magazine**", you simply say, "here is an article I wrote for **The Business Magazine.**" Both statements are 100% factual. Remember, the two key things about writing the article are, adding value and establishing credibility.

If you believe that writing articles is for you, set aside some time to (1) brainstorm which publications make sense for you to be in and (2) research the contact information of the editors of these publications so you can send articles to them once they have been written.

White Papers

White papers come in many forms, but the two most common white papers are some sort of research paper or something that is more of an editorial that adds value to the reader. If you were intimidated by the thought of writing a book, a white paper might be the ticket for you. White papers are longer than an article, but shorter than a book. Most white papers are between 5 and 20 pages. While White Papers cannot leverage Amazon for promotion, they still provide you an opportunity to establish your credibility and authority.

Let's say you wrote a White Paper entitled, *"21 Questions Physicians Need To Ask When Purchasing Disability Insurance."* You now have content that is incredibly valuable to physicians. So how do you use it in your prospecting efforts?

1. When you are referred to a physician and have scheduled an appointment, you can send him a copy of your white paper with a note that says, "looking forward to our meeting next Thursday. I have attached a white paper that I wrote that I know will give you some great information for our discussion." When the physician reads your white paper, he will instantly form an opinion of you. I cannot promise you that everyone is going you agree with your thoughts, but most will, and you will have differentiated yourself from your competition.

2. You could send the White Paper to selected COIs. You can then ask them, "who do you know that should be reading this white paper?"

3. If you are doing any direct marketing, you could include a copy of the white paper. Again, you will stand out from your competition.

4. Whenever you give a talk or presentation, offer to send your audience a copy of the white paper.

White papers are an alternative if you want to write more than an article, but don't want to write a book.

Blogs

I am sure that there are blogs that you currently read. If you read one or more on a consistent basis, it is probably because you find that the blog adds value to some aspect of your life. It could be in your personal life or in your business life, but the blogger is sharing ideas that resonate with you. So here is my question to you. Do you have thoughts and ideas that would add value to your prospects and clients? My guess is that your answer is yes.

What would be the impact if every week you shared one idea with your prospects, clients and Centers of Influence? Not a sales pitch, but rather an idea that adds value to their personal or business life. Emerson said, "if you want more, give more." I believe that a blog is a great way to give. And, I know from experience, that "giving" in a blog will lead to "getting" business.

So what does a blog really do for you? I believe it does three things. First, it shows that you are willing to give without expectation of something in return. Second, it establishes you as the expert in your field. And third, it keeps you top of mind. By reading your blog, people will get to know you and come to value your advice. Now that you are the recognized expert, when prospects, clients or Centers of Influence have a need, you are first person they think about. And, because you are continually posting a blog, they never forget about you. You will not lose sales because you came in a day, week or month too late. After all, how many times have you had a conversation with a prospect only to have them tell you, "we just bought your product through one of your competitors."

There are many platforms you can use to host your blog. Popular sites include Word Press, Blogger and Typepad. The key is to find one that you like and get started. My advice is to post at least once a week, so you can establish your credibility with your audience.

Two thinks you must know if you want to become a blogger.

1. Just because you build it, it does NOT mean they will come. Chances are nobody will read your blog unless you drive them to it. If you **DO** drive people to your blog, they **WILL** consume the content. The easiest way to get people to read or watch your blog is to send them a reminder. It could be the sole focus of an e-mail you send to them, or, it could be part of an e-newsletter you send to them.

2. Video blogs are the most popular blogs today. We would rather *watch* a video than *read* a short post. I know from personal experience that people love short 90 second to 2 minute video blogs. The good news is that the technology exists to make this process incredibly easy.

Once you start blogging, you can use it in your prospecting efforts like you would white papers and articles. Send it in advance of appointments, share it with COIs or use it in your direct marketing efforts.

Newsletters

For many companies and salespeople, the concept of mailing a physical newsletter has given way to the electronic version of newsletters, better known to us as e-newsletters. When e-newsletters were first introduced, they made a lot of sense. Back in the day, people were still excited to receive e-mails in their inbox. Additionally, there was a tremendous cost savings because there was no need for printing or postage.

E-newsletters continued to remain very effective until the e-mails we received on a daily basis began to overwhelm us. Instead of paying attention to each new e-mail, we now have to spend time deleting e-mails that are not mission critical. As a result, the open rate of e-newsletters has continually dropped to the point that the average open rate of e-newsletters hovers around 12-15%. So, while the concept may seem efficient, is it effective? Can you really afford to have your best prospects, clients and Centers of Influence continually delete the important messages in your e-newsletters without even reading them?

You should consider mailing, yes mailing, hard copy newsletters to your best prospects, clients and Centers of Influence. Here are two reasons why this **WILL** be effective.

First, nobody else is doing it! In all probability, you will be the only person/company in your space that is actually mailing a physical newsletter. This alone will make you stand out amongst your competitors.

Second, physical newsletters have "shelf life." When people receive the newsletter in the mail, they probably will not read it at that moment. But they will set it aside for later reading. When was the last time you set aside an e-mail to read later?

Now understand one thing. Your newsletter MUST add value. It cannot just be a promotion of you, your company and your products. If you add massive value, your targeted list WILL read your newsletter.

So, how often should you mail a physical newsletter? Ideally, once a month. But the reality is that you may need to ease into this. If you think this will be a challenge either from a content standpoint or a cost standpoint, start out doing it once a quarter. You can them move to every other month and then eventually move to monthly.

Earlier, I mentioned that you should mail to your best prospects, clients and COIs. I did not say you should mail to everyone. For example, let's say you have 5000 contacts in your database. In all probability you have between 250 and 500 that are your best clients, your high-target prospects and your key COIs. That is the group that you would mail to. This does two things. First, it makes sure you are effectively communicating with the true drivers of your business and second, it keeps costs down because you are not mailing to all 5000 contacts. I would continue to send your e-newsletter to all 5000 contacts. After all, some of them will eventually move into the top 250-500.

One last thing about newsletters. Make sure you have a Call-To-Action (CTA) in every newsletter. Examples of CTAs could be:

> Offering a free report
> Sign up for a free consultation
> Register for webinar or seminar

➤ Offering them a copy of your book
➤ Coupon for a discount on a product or service

These Calls-To-Action are critical because not only do they engage your audience, but it also allows you to measure the effectiveness of your mailings. By diligently tracking the responses and eventual business, you can determine the overall success of your mailings. Measuring the results of your marketing efforts are every bit as important as measuring other parts of your business.

E-Newsletters

E-newsletters are a great way deliver incredible value to your prospects, clients and Centers of Influence. When I speak of e-newsletters I am speaking of one-page or multiple page newsletters that are sent via e-mail.

I am old enough to remember the concept of the "blast fax." At the time, it seemed like the panacea of marketing. After all, you could create a newsletter and fax it to dozens, hundreds or thousands of people with just the push of the button. When I bought my first copy of WinFax, I thought I had died and gone to heaven. It seemed like the ultimate way to reach a mass amount of people with the least amount of effort.

In today's world, we can accomplish the same thing with "blast e-mails." By using services like Constant Contact, Aweber, Mail Chimp and iContact, we can send our electronic newsletter to dozens, hundreds or thousands of people. And the cost for these services is remarkably inexpensive.

E-newsletters allow you to remain top of mind for your prospects, clients and COIs. People are not going to respond to every e-mail you send out, but you do want them to think of you when they have a situation that you can help them with. I think it is critical that you add value in your e-mail marketing efforts. You want people to look forward to reading your newsletters instead of just deleting them. While many people use e-mail marketing to sell products and services, I believe you should add value before you ever try and sell something.

For those of you that ever did direct mail, you were taught that you cannot just mail one time and stop. You had to do it over and over before you got people's attention. The same is true with e-newsletters. You must be consistent in your delivery so people will recognize you. Whether you do it once a week or once a month, pick a frequency and stick to it.

I have done e-newsletters for many years and until recently tended to use a template provided by my service provider. While these templates are effective, in the research I have done, I am discovering that people don't feel special when they receive them. They do not feel you are personally talking to them, but instead view it as mass marketing. As a result, I am seeing more subject matter experts send out their newsletters in a format that is simply an e-mail. No fancy templates or graphics, just messages or ideas that have great content and add great value. Since it is going against the grain of what everybody else is doing, I do believe people are paying more attention to this format.

E-mail marketing that includes video is becoming incredibly popular. Think about how we are responding to YouTube. People simply like to watch videos. If you are not doing so already, you should consider using video links in your e-newsletter.

If you have not done so already, start collecting e-mail addresses so you can create a list to send your e-mails to. Don't worry if you have to start small. The key is getting started.

One final thought. Always remember that the reason to do any type of newsletter is to help you position yourself as an expert. It is not designed to be a commercial for how great you, your company or your product are.

Videos

Whether you personally like it or not, videos are changing the way we consume information and videos are changing the way people and companies are marketing to their customers.

People like videos so much that over 200 million hours of video are watched each and every day and those numbers are climbing exponentially.

The bottom line is that your prospects, clients and COIs actually WANT videos from you. Caveat, the videos they want are those that add value to them, not sales videos promoting you and your company. So always remember, VALUE, VALUE, VALUE.

I cannot think of a better way to introduce yourself to a massive amount of prospects than video. You get to make the exact, perfect impression each and every time. You tell them exactly what you want them to know without stumbling over words.

In all of your marketing efforts, both on-line and off-line you should be pointing your prospects to your videos. With your on-line marketing, you can send links to your videos.

Here is something that is a must. Once you have scheduled an appointment with a prospect for that initial meeting, send them a video. Your prospect will immediately form an impression of you and the path to making them a client will become so much shorter. I wish I could promise that everyone will fall in love with you, but even if they don't like what you say in the video, at least you can get them out of your pipeline quicker and instead focus your attention on true prospects.

Videos are a great addition to websites. Also, if you are doing a blog, consider using videos in your blog. It will dramatically increase the number of people who actually consume the information.

When we think of videos, we almost always think of YouTube. Check out these numbers:

> 1 Billion people use YouTube
> 4 Billion videos are viewed each day on YouTube
> 6 Billion hours of video are watched each month on YouTube
> 300 hours of new video are upload each minute on YouTube
> 1 Billion YouTube videos are viewed each day on a mobile device

With numbers like this, doesn't it make sense to tap into this phenomenon? And the good news is that YouTube wants to help you do this. You can create a channel on YouTube, and YouTube wants your content so bad, that they offer you this opportunity for **FREE**. Imagine, your own channel with all of your videos.

Now, YouTube is certainly not the only platform for your videos. Many people use services like Vimeo to post their videos. My recommendation is to post them in both places. Platforms like YouTube and Vimeo allow your prospects, clients and COIs to receive great value from you because they have a place to go to consume the information that interests them.

When you post multiple videos, people really get you know you and what you stand for. It allows you to develop and deepen relationships so much quicker.

Make sure you optimize your videos for SEO searches by including keywords in the description of your videos. Videos will move you and your company up higher in the search engine rankings than any other thing you do. The primary reason is because Google owns YouTube and loves promoting YouTube. Caveat, you can pay Google to get higher placements, but video is the best way to do it for free.

Right now there are very few companies and salespeople taking advantage of this opportunity. By having videos in your marketing efforts, you will truly stand out from your competitors.

Before I close, let me address the most common question I receive regarding videos. It sounds something like this, "Chris, what camera should I buy?" The answer might be, don't buy one! Look, you can have your videos done professionally or you can shoot them with your iPhone. Your iPhone will produce great quality videos. My recommendation however, is to make sure you get an external microphone and hook up to the iPhone. What ruins most videos is not the camera, but instead poor sound quality. Spend $49 for a lavaliere mike that you can connect to your iPhone and hook up on your shirt and can start producing great videos to help you in your prospecting efforts.

And another thing to consider. You don't have to be on camera to produce a video. If for whatever reason you don't want to be on camera, just create a PowerPoint or Keynote presentation and then add your narration. My advice here is the same as if you are in front of the camera. Make sure you use a good microphone to insure good sound quality.

Webinars

Now, you might be asking yourself, how are webinars related to publishing? My experience with webinars is that many people have conflicts when you are conducting your live webinar, yet want to consume your content. By recording the webinar, you allow people to view it at their convenience, when they are in the mind-set to listen to your message. So, in effect, you are publishing your webinar to a site that your prospects can access.

But, let's back up a moment. You are probably thinking, why webinars?

I think you will agree that it is becoming increasingly challenging to get prospects to attend events these days. More and more of them are turning to the Internet for information. A webinar is a perfect way to take advantage of this. You can add tremendous value with a great webinar.

With webinars, you can talk to a few, or you can talk to many. And the good news is that you do not have to worry about how many people eventually show up. If you are holding an event at a conference center or a hotel, you are always worried about room cost, room setup and how no shows will affect your cost. There is no such worry with a webinar.

You can sponsor your own webinar. You will create the content, market the webinar and deliver the webinar.

You could co-sponsor a webinar in which you have another person or organization market the webinar and possibly be a co-presenter with you.

You could be a guest on somebody else's webinar and market to your prospects.

Whichever avenue you choose, the key thing to remember about a webinar is that it is designed first and foremost to add value. It should not be a sales presentation. Your prospects will be engaged if there is something in it for them. They will leave the webinar if they feel the only thing you are doing on the webinar is selling them.

In your webinar, it is critical that you have some type of a Call-To-Action. Maybe you want them to download a PDF. Maybe you want them to schedule an appointment with you. What your Call-To-Action is not as important to actually having one. Remember, the people who attend your webinar are becoming "hot" prospects, so take the next step with them.

As I mentioned earlier, make sure you record the webinar so those that did not attend the live version can view it at their convenience. Make sure you send the re-play link to all those that registered but did not show up. You can also send the link to everyone on your list and let them view it if the topic is of interest to them.

Some people record a webinar that they did not invite anybody to. They then take that recording and send it to their list or post it on their website. The beauty of webinars is that your have so much flexibility for basically no cost.

For those of you who have not dipped your toes into the webinar waters, there are several options you can use to produce and promote your webinars.

A great source to use is Google. Google Hangouts is free. All you need is a Gmail address.

With Google Hangouts, you can have an unlimited amount of attendees. You could have hundreds or thousands of people on your webinar and there is no charge to you.

The cool thing about using Google Hangouts is that you are taking advantage of the Google platform, which adds credibility.

I am by no means suggesting that Google Hangouts is the only platform, or, that it is the best platform. There are other vendors out there like Go-To-Meeting. GTM allows you to have 25 guests on the webinar with you. If you routinely exceed that number, you might have to upgrade to Go-To-Webinar.

Adobe is another vendor you could use. Many people use WebEx to host their webinars. You can use join.me.

Keep in mind that GTM, Adobe and WebEx all charge for their services. You need to compare the features and costs to determine what is right for you.

I also want to tell you about an incredible program called Webinar Jam. This service is really the front end and back end of your webinar and integrates with Google Hangouts. It takes care of all the scheduling, reminders, follow-ups and recordings of your webinars. If you are planning to make webinars a big part of your practice, you should research this program.

I passionately believe that webinars are a great way for you to establish credibility with prospects and Centers of Influence. It is flexible, convenient, efficient and incredibly cost effective.

Virtual Summits

If you are like me, you have been to numerous live seminars and conferences. Some of these were held in your city, some required you to travel to attend. During those events, you were exposed to education and ideas from the featured speakers. In all probability, you had the option to pick and choose which sessions you wanted to attend. Imagine for a second if you could replicate the education and ideas without the hassle of travel. That is what a Virtual Summit can do. It is basically an on-line conference. The speakers are the same. The education and ideas are the same. The difference is that you attend virtually (on your computer) instead of attending live. These Virtual Summits can be a 1-day event or a multiple-day event.

Now I am not trying to say that live seminars and conferences are not valuable. They certainly are. There is nothing like talking and socializing face-to-face. But the reality is that travel is becoming more of hassle than ever before and companies continue to tighten their belts in terms of T&E budgets. This is why Virtual Summits can be a great alternative.

Now, I am not going to go into great details about how to organize and produce a Virtual Summit. My friend, Michal Alf, has written a great book on that subject. Check out his book on Amazon, ***The Virtual Summit Formula: How Your Virtual Summit Can Attract Thousands Of Participants, Grow Your Email List and Boost Your Business.***

Instead, I want to give you two ideas on how you can use a Virtual Summit in your prospecting efforts to establish enormous credibility and create countless highly-qualified, highly-motived prospects for your pipeline.

The first idea is when your targeted prospects are the "end users" of the Virtual Summit. The second idea is when your targeted prospects are the "speakers" on the Virtual Summit.

Here is an example for targeting prospects who are going to be the "end users" of the Virtual Summit. In other words, they are going to log onto their computers and consume the information provided by the speakers. Let's say you are a financial planner and your target market is dentists. You can take the lead on creating a Virtual Summit (maybe even be the sponsor of the Summit) and line up speakers who can give great value to dentist. You could title your summit, *"Grow Your Practice, Grow Your Life: How To Double The Revenue of Your Practice With Less Hours, Less Overhead, While Having More Time Off."* Obviously, your speakers would be experts that have worked with dentists in making this happen (please don't focus on this title or idea, it is just a sample. Focus on ideas you can create).

I would suggest that you are also a featured speaker on the Summit. Again, Michael Alf's book can go into the details of a successful summit, but one thing I do want to point out. Each of the speakers will send e-mails to their list to drive attendance. In this case, the combine mailing list of all the speakers could be in the thousands or tens of thousands.

The second example is when you are targeting potential speakers for your summit. Let's say you are an attorney who has a specialty as a Cyber Breach Coach. These are the "go to" people when a company has a cyber security breach. Typically, these Cyber Breach Coaches want to establish relationships with insurance carriers and CTOs/CIOs of companies. So in this case, you invite key people within insurance companies and key CTOs/CIOs to be speakers for your summit. By giving these people a platform to speak, you are creating great value for them. The relationship that you can develop and deepen through this process is hard to duplicate. Like the previous example, you could be a speaker and a sponsor.

The opportunity to repurpose this content in your marketing and prospecting efforts are enormous.

The concept of a Virtual Summit combines some of the ideas I mentioned in other parts of this book, specifically the sections on Speaking and Podcasting.

If you need help creating a Virtual Summit, visit my website at www.prospectingthroughpositioning.com

Webcasts

A medium that is growing at an incredible pace is Webcasting. Webcasts are similar to Webinars, but they take the engagement to a deeper level with the audience.

The best way to describe a Webcast is that it is an on-line TV show. Where webinars typically feature a PowerPoint or Keynote presentation, Webcasts involve the use of a video camera(s) where the host is on screen. It could be as simple as the host using the camera built into his/her computer, or, it could involve several cameras that will show several angles of the set.

Unlike TV, Webcasts give you the ability to engage with your audience in real time. Through the use of a chat feature, you can instantly receive feedback from those that are watching. This ability does not exist with television. Imagine the impact when you can get immediate feedback when you are doing your live show!

And, with platforms like Google Hangouts, you can stream your show to just a few people or to thousands of people. The best part? These platforms are absolutely free! Just as FYI, there are numerous "paid" services that allow you to stream your show. You just need to determine which is best for you.

Podcasting

I am sure many of you are already listening to podcasts. For those of you who are not, the best way to describe a podcast is that it is an Internet radio show. Each episode may only last a few minutes, or, an episode may last 30, 45 or 60 minutes. The great thing about a podcast is that you are the owner, the producer and the star of the show. Your podcast can be on any topic you are passionate about.

I believe that podcasting is important for two reasons. First, it is one of the easiest and best ways to establish your credibility in any market. Second, podcasting is a phenomenal prospecting tool (I will go into more detail later).

In the last two years, there has been an incredible explosion in the number of podcast that are being created. In my opinion, the two main reasons this explosion is occurring are (1) how easy it is to launch a podcast and (2) the different places that people can consume the podcast.

When I say easy, I really mean **super-easy**. In fact, one of the world's leading companies stands ready to help you. You can use the Apple platform in your podcasting efforts. Apple, specifically iTunes, is the platform on which the over-whelming majority of podcasts are listened to. So, Apple will host your podcast.

Not only that, but Apple will promote your podcast. And, Apple will do all this for free. Think about what I just described. One of the world's leading companies is standing by to help you establish immense credibility, help you in your prospecting efforts and will not charge you for these services. That is the kind of help I want!

But Apple is not the only place where people are consuming podcasts. There are also services like Stitcher, iHeartRadio, Pandora and Google Play where you can listen to podcasts.

While those are the locations that people go to find the podcast, it is important to keep in mind that podcasts can be listened to on any device. You can listen to a podcast on your desktop, laptop, tablet or smart phone. And, almost all automobile manufactures are building the different podcast platforms into the entertainment devices that are installed in their cars. So, you no longer have to connect your smart phone to the entertainment device in your car to be able to listen to your favorite podcast.

The average commute in the United States is 27 minutes. It is not a coincidence that many of the top podcasters target their shows for 30 minutes so they can take advantage of this. Imagine the impact of your prospecting and marketing efforts when you have prospects, clients and Centers of Influence listening to your podcast on their way to and from work!

I talk to many people who listen to podcasts when they are working out. I personally listen to my favorite podcasts when I am traveling. I download the podcasts to my iPad, then, when I get settled into my seat on the plane, I start listening to the podcasts. Not only does it make the time seem to fly by (I could not resist that one), but I fill my head with great messages and ideas.

OK, you are probably saying to yourself, "Chris tell me how I can use podcasting in my marketing efforts. Here is how you do it:

The Basics

> ➤ The content of your podcast must create massive value for your target market. It is not a podcast about you, but rather a podcast about things that can help them.
> ➤ The podcast is not about you selling you your services.
> ➤ You need to determine how often you are going to post an episode. My recommendation is weekly.
> ➤ The best way to get in front of prospect with podcasting? Invite them to be a guest on your show. This gives you a great opportunity to develop a new relationship or deepen an existing relationship. The key to this is no selling. Let the relationship develop naturally. You will have an opportunity at a later date to approach them about your services. But I will promise you that many of the people you interview will ask you about your services.

Great Example

Let's say you live in Dallas and your target market is business owners of small to medium sized companies. What if you were to create a podcast called Dallas Business Weekly and you interviewed Presidents and CEOs of successful companies in the Dallas areas? This podcast is about business, not about the product or service you sell.

In your first few episodes, you interview prominent business owners that you already have a relationship with. This gets the momentum started.

Now, you are going to reach out to other business owners, those that would be ideal clients for you.

The easiest way to approach those business owners is to get a referral from a current client or current Center of Influence. Assuming these people know what your ideal client looks like, simply ask, "John, who do you think I should invite to be a guest on my show?" The fact that you have a show will engage their brain like no other. You will be amazed at the people they will come up with and you will be even more amazed about how hard they will work to get those people to agree to be a guest on your show. You have just created your show's sales force.

But there are going to be prospects that you are targeting that no one in your network is connected to. So, instead of picking up the phone and trying to make a cold call, you can now send a letter in an Express Mail envelope inviting the business owner to be a guest on your show. When they read the prominent business owners who have already appeared on your show, your ability to book them on your show will be easier than you think.

Once they have agreed to be a guest, arrange a pre-interview session. The purpose of the session is to make them feel comfortable about the questions and help them be prepared to answer the questions. This session could be over the phone, but if possible, I would do it in person, since it is a great way to establish a relationship with him/her. Once they are comfortable with the upcoming interview, schedule the day/time you are going to do the actual interview.

I would recommend that you conduct the interview in one of two ways. The ideal way is to conduct the interview in person. You can use a hand held recorder (think the recorders that sports reporters use to conduct post game interviews in the locker room), download BossJock to your phone or tablet and record on that, or bring your laptop and use a program like Audacity to record the interview. If you are going to use anything but a hand held recorder, make sure you attach a quality microphone to your phone, tablet or laptop.

If you are unable to conduct the interview in person, then use Skype to do the interview. You don't *have* to use the video component of Skype, because you are most concerned with the audio. If you are using a Mac, the best way to record your call is using a program called *ecamm call recorder.* If you are using a PC, the best way to record you call is using a program called *Pamela*. Both of the programs cost about $29.

In the actual interview, you ask your guest questions like how they got started, what challenges they overcame, what challenges they are facing today and what challenges they see in the future. Just a conversation where they can give great tips that will help other business owners.

Now that the interview is complete, you can do your edits and add any intros or outros. Then, upload the episode and your podcast is live for all to consume.

Remember, up until this point, you have not talked about you, your product or your services.

About a week after you have posted the interview, I would recommend that you arrange to stop by the interviewee's office. Bring them something as a way of thanking them. Maybe it is a framed logo of your podcast that says, thanks to Bill Austin, Austin Manufacturing, Episode #23. Simply give the framed picture to Bill and say, "Bill, I just wanted to thank you for being a guest on my show. Here is a small token of my appreciation. We have received great feedback on the interview, so I am going to send you the link to the interview and the actual MP3 file that you can share with your prospects, clients and Centers of Influence. In fact, many previous guests actually put it on their website."

Think for a moment about the impact this can have for you and your show. All of your guests are sharing their interview with their network. It is like dropping a rock in the lake and watching the ripples across the water. You can exponentially grow your contact list as a result.

As a reminder, you have yet to talk about you, your product or your services.

A week or two after you deliver the framed logo, give Bill a call (this will no longer be a cold call!) to make sure he received your e-mail with the link to your podcast and the MP3 file. **Now** is the time you can transition to talking about you and your products. Let's make the assumption that you are an Insurance Advisor who specializes in Employee Benefits. Before you hang up you can say, "Bill, one of the things we did not discuss is what I do. I specialize in providing employee benefits to companies in the Metroplex. What objection would you have if I contacted the person in your company who handles this?" Now, I am not here to promise that you will make every sale, but I will promise that you will have immense credibility by the time you ask that question.

In reality, your interviewee will probably ask what you do for a living somewhere along this process. You can certainly answer the question, but your challenge is not to default into "sales mode." Establish the credibility before you try to sell anything.

I will give you three reasons why I like podcasting so much. (1) I get to talk to the type of people I am most interested in, (2) I am adding a ton of value (regardless of how many sales I make) and (3) it is flat out fun to create, produce and distribute.

Look, I know podcasting is not for everyone, but it is a great avenue if you want to come in above the line of credibility and make prospecting so much easier.

Writing A Book

Few people would argue that the #1 way to be known as the expert in your market niche is to write a book. This is true in every industry I know of. It is not a coincidence that author is contained in the word authority. Become an author and you become an authority.

OK, let's hit the pause button for just a second. Many of you are probably thinking, "Chris, I don't have the time to sit down and write a book." But here is my challenge to you. How many hours do you currently waste on prospecting methods that producer little or no results? You might be having lots of motion, but producing very little progress. What would happen if you took that one hour of ineffective cold calling and instead spent one hour towards your book? My guess is that within 60-90 days you would have a book!

When it comes to writing a book:

- ➤ You can write the book
- ➤ You can co-author the book with one person or possibly many people
- ➤ You can hire a ghost-writer
- ➤ If you have a blog, you can compile your best blogs into a book
- ➤ If you have a podcast, you can compile your best episodes into a book
- ➤ You can be interviewed and turn that interview into a great book. In fact, there are companies out there that will actually do all the heavy lifting. They will interview you and turn that interview into a book

Keep something very important in mind. You are not writing the book to win a Pulitzer Prize. Rather, you are writing a book that adds value to those that you serve and which you can use in your prospecting efforts. So don't worry about being a great writer. Most books being written today by Subject Matter Experts (SMEs) are not 200-300 page books. In fact, most of the books that are becoming best sellers are between 60 and 120 pages. You can have more pages, but you do not need to in order for the book to provide great value to your targeted reader.

Here are some helpful hints as you start thinking about writing a book. I am obviously not writing a book on "how to write a book," so these are just some things that I have learned through research, talking with best selling authors and personal experience. There are countless resources available to you that go into great detail of writing a book.

Getting Started

One of my favorite sayings is, "you don't have to be great to get started, but you have to get started to be great." So, the key is to get started on your book. As I mentioned earlier, there are several ways you can write a book. But for this section, I am going to assume that you are "going it alone" with no co-authors and you are not repurposing other content for your book (i.e. your best blog post or your transcribed podcasts).

I think there are five initial steps you need to take in regards to your book. They are:

- ➤ Determine the subject of your book
- ➤ Create the title of your book
- ➤ Create the outline of your book
- ➤ Determine if you are going to write or dictate your book

> ➢ Set a deadline for completion of your book

1. Determine The Subject Of Your Book: This is where it all begins, what do you want to write about? If your thought process is to write a book that you can use in your prospecting and marketing efforts, keep one very important thing in mind. You must write the book for your readers, not for yourself. In other words, look at the book through their "lenses" not yours. That may seem obvious, but I have talked to numerous individuals who are way too "me" centered and therefore their message falls flat.

Given your expertise and given the niche you are targeting, what can you write about that would give value to your readers (prospects, clients and Centers of Influence). Always remember, the two main purposes of your book are (1) provide value and (2) position yourself as an authority.

I believe that the best subject of your book is the solution to your target market's biggest problem. If you help them solve their biggest problem (or it least start them on that path) you will be "above the line of credibility" and can engage with these readers on an entirely different level than your competitors.

2. Create The Title Of Your Book: The title of your book is critical to capture the attention of your target market. When a person hears or sees the title of your book, you want her to say, "that's me," or "that's what I have been struggling with," or "that's exactly what I have been thinking." My advice to be informative and creative without being too cute. Cute does not sell, information and value does.

So, once you know the subject of your book, take some time to brainstorm the title. Find a quiet place, a place that inspires your creative thinking. Take out a yellow pad and just start writing down all kinds of titles. Write down dozens of titles. Nothing should be considered crazy or stupid at this point. Take a break and then come back to the titles and start picking out the ones that truly capture your message. You will be surprised at how easy the "cream rises to the top." Eventually you will narrow your choice to two or three and then eventually choose the one you will go with. This is not a race, so take your time in determining your title.

Once you have the title, you then need to go through the same process to create your sub-title. Think of it this way. The title captures people's attention, then the sub-title really connects with the person and tells them what the book is about.

3. Create The Outline Of Your Book: The outline of your book is similar to the architect's drawing of a house. You need to have an idea of what the final product will look like. Once you have the outline, you will be amazed at how easy it is to start writing. My experience is that with a great outline, writing your book becomes a "fill in the blank" exercise. You already know the subject of a particular section or chapter, so now you just fill it up!

4. Determine If You Are Going To Write Or Dictate Your Book: You might be thinking that the only way to "write" a book is to sit down at your computer and start typing. For many, that is the best way for them to get the book done. But you can also "record" yourself and then have the recording transcribed for you. Here are a couple things to consider when making this decision.

I am a visual, so "seeing" things is the way I process information and, therefore, help me with my creativity. As a result, I chose to write (type) my book. It worked for me on my <u>first book</u> and it worked for me in writing this book.

You might be an auditory, so "hearing" things is the way you process information and, therefore, that helps you with your creativity. If this is the case, you can choose to dictate your book. All you have to do is find your favorite device (iPhone or portable recorder) and start talking. Now, you should have some clarity and direction of what you are going to talk about during each of these sessions, but just press record and start talking. There is a great tool out there called <u>Rev</u> that you can download to your smartphone. Just press record and it will capture your audio. What makes <u>Rev</u> such a great product is you can immediately push "transcribe" and the service will transcribe your audio into Word format. You can use these transcriptions to compile and edit the final copy of your book.

If you happen to give a lot of talks, presentations or training sessions, consider recording those that contain the content you want to include in your book. Again, get the recording transcribed and you will quickly fill up the pages of your book. I know several authors whose book is basically a transcription of one of their presentations, since what they cover in their presentation is the exact information they want to have in a book.

5.   Set A Deadline For Completion Of Your Book: Nothing motivates a writer more than a deadline. I cannot tell you what your deadline should be, but I can tell you that you need to have a deadline. Keep this in mind. The sooner you write and publish the book, the sooner you can use it in your prospecting efforts. It is my belief that you can have your book completed within 12 weeks. To do this, you must be disciplined to set aside a small amount of time each day to write between 250 and 500 words. As I have mentioned earlier, you can find this time by *not* doing some of the unproductive prospecting activity you are currently doing and invest that time into your book.

Publishing Your Book

While you could go through the hassles and expense of what I call "old school" publishing, there really is no need to. Today, there are so many easy ways to self publish. My advice would be to look to Amazon for your publishing needs.

Amazon has a service called Create Space that you can use to self publish your book. It is an incredibly easy platform to use and is what I used to publish not only this book, but also my previous book, Unique Sales Wisdom. Once you have completed your book, to include the front and back cover, all you have to do is upload all of this within your Create Space account. Then, typically within 48 hours, your book will be available for purchase on Amazon! And consider what Amazon will do for you once this book is on the site:

> ➢ Amazon will promote your book.
> ➢ Amazon will print, sell and deliver your book
> ➢ Amazon will pay you when people buy the book
> ➢ Amazon will give you a dedicated author page on Amazon.com

Back in the "old school" publishing days, you had to buy hundreds or thousands of copies of your book and hope you could sell them. Now, with print on demand technology, you do not have to fill your garage with unsold books!

And the best news? Amazon does not charge you anything for all of this. That's right, you can get all these services from Amazon for free!

Marketing Your Book

An entire book could be written on how to market your book, but for now, I just want to give a few high level ideas about marketing your book. When I talk about marketing your book, what I am referring to is getting your book recognized as a best seller, which will make you a best selling author. Think about the credibility you will have with your targeted audience when you are known as a #1 Best Selling Author. It will be a game changer for you.

In the most simplest of terms, what you need to do is pick a launch date for your book and begin marketing that date to your lists of contacts and also ask others for help in marketing your book to their lists. Let's say you are going to launch your book on June 1. A few weeks before that, you would start letting your list know that your book is going to be released on June 1 and they should be on the lookout for special bonuses that they will receive when they buy the book on that date. In other words, create some buzz and some anticipation. At the same time, you need to arm those that are going to announce your book to their list with all the copy and links so it is so easy for them to promote your book.

Then on June 1, everybody e-mails their list with the announcement of your book. Get people posting on LinkedIn, Twitter, Facebook and Websites. You want as many people as possible buying the book within a 24-hour window so you can drive sales within your category. Done correctly, most people can achieve a #1 Best Seller status.

This is just a high level explanation. My advice is to not go this alone. Work with an expert to make sure you accomplish your goals. Your return on investment will be through the roof.

Prospecting With Your Book

Since this *IS* a book on prospecting, we need to talk about how you use your book in your prospecting efforts. Here are 6 ideas you can use.

1. Book As Your Business Card: When your competition meets with a prospect, they typically hand them a card. Image the difference when you hand your prospect a copy of your book. Going forward, your book will be your business card, so make sure you have copies with you at all times. Let's face it, business cards get thrown away almost immediately. Your book will have shelf life.

I believe the key to this process is the follow up. When you give someone a business card, rarely do you follow up and ask, "what did you think of my business card?" With a book, you have a license to follow up! You can call or e-mail the person you gave the book to and ask, "did you get a chance to glance at the book? Make sure you read Chapter 4 because it is exactly what we talked about when we met." This process allows you to add value and deepen the relationship. I wish I could tell you that every prospect is going to call you back immediately and tell you that they want to do business with you. Obviously that will not be the case. But you are positioning yourself as the authority and have begun the process of eliminating your competition. As you continue to market to this person, you will be at the top of the list when they become a "right now" buyer.

2. Giving Away Books At Your Speaking Engagements: When your competition does a seminar, they give the audience a copy of their slides. When you do a seminar, you give your audience a copy of your book. Who wins?

By giving away books at your speaking engagements, you are combining two of the three critical action items to come in above the line of credibility, publishing and speaking. No matter how good your talk is, people will quickly forget as they get back to their daily grind. Giving them a book is a constant reminder of your expertise. Like I mentioned with the business card, make sure you follow up to find out if they glanced or read the book.

It is critical that you capture the names and contact information of the people who attend your talk. Sometimes the sponsor of the event will provide you with this information. If that is not available, make sure you use technology that easily allows you to capture this information. I use an amazing tool called Instant Customer that allows me to not only capture the contact information, but also sets up autoresponders so I can send out several pieces of information automatically (with no additional work on my part). So think about what can happen. You give a talk that gives great value. You give attendees a copy of your book that adds great value. Then you automatically send them additional content that gives them great value. That, my friends, is positioning.

3. Using Books With Your Centers Of Influence (COIs): There are two scenarios where you can use your book with COIs. First, is when you are trying to **develop** a relationship with a COI. Second, is when you already know the COI and want to **deepen** the relationship.

Let's talk first about developing a relationship with a COI. In all probability, you are targeting the same potential COIs as your competition. All of you are trying to convince these COIs that you are the person they should introduce their clients and contacts to. But the reality is that these COIs are asking themselves, "what makes this person any different than all the others that are asking me for referrals?" So what is that difference? Everyone talks about how good their product or service is, how hard they are going to work and how competitive their pricing is. In the COI's mind, there is little or no difference.

But now you come along and give this COI a copy of your book. You are the only person with a book. You have established credibility and are in a position to ask for referrals and introductions much sooner than ever before.

The second scenario is where you already have a relationship with a COI and want to deepen the relationship. The first step is to give them a copy of the book and ask them to read the book and give you feedback. Since you know the book adds value, their response is almost always favorable. Once you follow up and get their feedback, you now ask the magical question, "who do you know that I should send this book to?" Ask if they can write a short note and attach the note to the front of the book. It might be something like, "Bob, here is a book you should read. Chris has done a great job in explaining the issues you are dealing with." You can then mail the book on their behalf.

Now let's put this idea on steroids. Once they write the note, you can ask your COI to send a short e-mail to their contact telling them that a book is on the way AND introducing you as the author. You are now in a position to follow up after this person has received the book. This is the ultimate win-win-win. The COI wins because he is giving their contact (client?) a book. You win because you receive an introduction. The person you are referred to wins because they have a valuable book.

Now let's put this idea on Human Growth Hormones. Instead of asking the COI, "who do you know that I should send this book to," you come prepared with a list of names of people you want to be introduced to. People that your COI knows. The conversation goes like this. "Dave, I am targeting a few select people as key prospects for my business. Take a look at this 3x5 card. Which of the people on the card should I send this book to?" You will find out more about these prospects and then you can follow the process of note, e-mail introduction, mail the book and follow up.

When you follow up with the people you are referred to (and you *do* have to follow up), the conversation is on a whole different level than any conversation you have had in the past. You are talking from a position of authority and instead of trying to beg for an appointment, you can now determine if you even want to meet with them. You have completely flipped who is in control of the process.

So my question to you is, how many "book referrals" would you need to absolutely rock your world?

4. Sending Books In Advance Of Your Initial Meeting:
The first meeting with a prospect is like a first date. Neither person really knows what to expect and

sometimes the conversation can be awkward because of lack of familiarity.

Ideally, you would like your prospect to feel that they already know you and like you, before that first meeting. Sending them a copy of your book in advance of that first meeting could be the key to accomplishing this. So, regardless of how you obtained this first appointment (referral, speaking engagement, direct mail, on-line, etc.), my suggestion is to send them a copy of your book in advance of your meeting. You can send it via Federal Express or use Express Mail from the Post Office. Using either of these two methods will almost always guarantee that the package gets directly to your prospect and that he/she will open it personally.

You can write a personal note that says, "Susan, looking forward to our meeting on the 23rd. Here is a copy of my book that I hope you find helpful." BAM, instant credibility! I promise you that none of your competitors are doing this. And, now Susan has the opportunity to learn more about you and your philosophy before that "first date."

Once you do have that first meeting, it is so easy to ask Susan if she had an opportunity to read, or at least skim, the book. You are cementing your authority status. Now, this act alone does not guarantee you will get the business, but I promise that it **does** speed up the sales cycle.

If you choose to send the books personally, you can order multiple copies of the book from Create Space and you pay the discounted author's rate for each copy of the book. Depending on the number of pages in your book, the typical cost is between $2 - $3 per copy. If you want to take advantage of the full technology of Amazon, you could order the book from Amazon, type in your note and

Amazon will ship the book on your behalf. In this case you would be paying the retail price. But, if you are an Amazon Prime Member (and therefore have free shipping), the net-net cost to you might actually be cheaper than mailing the book yourself. The biggest difference in that the note is typed by Amazon instead of a personal hand-written note.

5. Send Books To Your Target 100: Almost every salesperson I know has a Top 100 list of what I call Dream Prospects. These are the prospects they would die to have. The biggest challenge is the all of their competitors feel the same way and are also targeting these great prospects. Not only that, the incumbent provider does not want to lose this great prospect, so he/she is probably lavishing great service upon them.

Getting through all of this clutter is certainly a challenge. Sending a book to each of these targeted prospects might be the key to getting that first appointment that has been elusive in the past. You can use the same techniques I described in the previous section. My question for you is, how many of these Target 100 prospects do you need to convert to a client to make this a great year? My guess is not many, so why not invest the time and money to leverage your book as a way to get that first appointment?

But here is a bonus idea for you. On your letter or note, tell this great prospect that you are writing a second book and it is going to contain interviews with thought leaders in the *(insert your niche)* industry. Tell them that you would love for him/her to be one of those interviews and you would like to set up a time to discuss the book project.

Now, obviously you need to be writing this second book. When you meet with the prospect, you can only talk about the book and the interview you would like to do. There is no selling at this point, that will come later. By having this introductory meeting and then the subsequent interview, you are establishing not only creditability but also a relationship. You could take this a step further if you have a podcast, by having this prospect as a guest on your show.

My second bonus idea for you is to transcribe the podcast interview and make *that* the interview you put in your book. By re-purposing the podcast interview, you are leveraging you time and efforts.

After you have done the interviews, you now can approach the prospect about what you do. But my guess is that he/she will have already initiated that conversation during this process.

6. Using Social Media: Now you may, or may not, be someone who uses Social Media in your prospecting and marketing efforts. If you are, I have an idea you can use. If you are not, I have an idea you can use.

Let's start with an idea if you are *not* using Social Media in your sales and prospecting efforts. On the home page of your website, offer to give away the PDF version of your book for free. All the person has to do is provide their contact information and you will send them the PDF version. You can ask for as little or as much information as you want. After all, you are giving them something of value for free.

It should not come as a surprise that the more information you ask for, the fewer opt-ins you will get. But, those that give you all of that information are potentially much better prospects for you. If, on the other hand, all you ask for is first name and e-mail address, your opt-in rate will be much higher.

Technology today makes this process so easy. You can set up an auto-responder that will automatically send the PDF version of your book when the person opts-in. Then that e-mail address is added to your e-mail/e-newsletter database so you can market to them in the future.

If you **are** using social media in your prospecting and marketing efforts, in addition to having a link on your website, you can offer this free PDF version of your book on LinkedIn and/or Facebook. The same procedure to get the book applies to the LinkedIn and Facebook opt-in as with the website opt-in.

Now, you might be thinking, "Chris, why do I want to give my book away for free?" Keep this in mind. You are not going to make any substantial amount of money selling your book. But, you can make a substantial amount of money by giving your book away to prospects and then convert those prospects into clients.

My final recommendation regarding the free PDF version, don't make this offer until you have done your initial marketing launch of the book.

Writing An E-Book

You can probably tell from the previous section on using a Book in your prospecting efforts that I am very passionate about the importance of you writing a book and using it in your prospecting and marketing efforts. But I am also a realist and know that you may not want to go through all the steps of publishing a physical book. If you fall into that category, you might want to consider an E-book. E-books are typically shorter than a "printed/published" book and sometimes that is the reason you might be thinking of going down this path.

An E-Book stills give you the platform to establish yourself as a thought leader in your niche. Your E-Book can add great value to your prospects, clients and Centers of Influence. And, it can be produced without any of the extra work required to actually publish a physical book.

Once you have completed your E-Book, you can use many of the same marketing techniques that I described in the previous section. While you will have success with an E-Book, right or wrong, it is not nearly as powerful as that physical book. If you are not sure you want to commit to publishing a physical book, give some thought to taking that first step with an E-Book.

Here is hint for you. Writing the book is much harder than getting a physical book published. With just a little extra effort, you will multiply your returns.

Direct Mail

The question that is often asked is, "how do I get people to want all this stuff I am publishing?"

This requires a two-part answer. The first part is that you should assume that your current clients, targeted prospects and Centers of Influence will be interested in valuable information that you can share with them that will help them. So, we are going to make sure that whatever we publish, they get.

The second part of the answer is that we need to create marketing opportunities that allow all the other suspects to raise their hand and say, "I want to start a conversation with you." The way you do this is through Direct Response Marketing. Now, there are volumes of entire books written on Direct Response Marketing and this will not be one of them. However, it is critical that (1) you understand the basics of Direct Response Marketing and (2) you implement Direct Response in your marketing plan.

In its simplest form, Direct Response Marketing is when you mail, e-mail, do a Facebook ad, do a radio ad, television ad, magazine ad or newspaper ad and you ask the prospect to respond. Respond to receive something like a white paper, free report, sample product or consultation. In other words, they respond, they get something. It is in effect, an ethical bribe. You are bribing them with something of value in order to receive their contact information. Once you receive this contact information, you can then put them into a marketing funnel in which you continue to communicate with them as they move down the buy line. In this funnel, you are probably sending them additional value add pieces to continue to establish your credibility.

At this point you might be thinking, "but I do not want to do direct mail." Keep in mind that Direct Response Marketing is not limited to snail mail. As I just mentioned, you can use other mediums like e-mail, radio, television, magazines, newspapers or social media in your efforts. The key is to use the medium that your ideal customers are paying attention to.

But, with so much emphasis being geared toward on-line marketing, results from direct mail are better than ever. The reason? Our in-boxes for our e-mail accounts are overflowing with messages. People feel overwhelmed and are ignoring most messages and almost always ignore marketing messages. Conversely, our regular mailbox is not as full as it used to be. That means that if you are doing direct mail, there is not much competition for your prospect's attention.

Another thought that might be running through your head is, "but I hear response rates are really low, like 1-4%." The response rate depends on two critical factors. First, the quality of copy of your message and second, the quality of your offer. If you have a kick ass message and a kick ass offer, you can experience great response rates. But the response rate, be it high or be it low, is not the key metric. Instead, you need to measure the revenue that is generated from the campaign. For example, if you spent $2000 on a direct mail campaign and that campaign generated $80,000 in revenue, would you be upset if only 3% of the people you sent the letter to responded?

My guess is that you would be ecstatic, not upset and you would be looking for ways to spend another $2000 so you can repeat this fantastic ROI. True marketing professionals will tell you that dollars spent on Direct Response Marketing is the best, most predictable marketing dollars you can spend. If you want to master this craft and create a steady stream of money coming into your company, read anything you can by Dan Kennedy, Frank Kern and Joe Polish. They are some of the true masters of Direct Response Marketing.

One final thought. There are giants in the e-commerce world that are using direct mail to drive their prospects to their websites. Think about that. Some of the very best "on-line" companies are using "off-line" tactics to create sales. Maybe you should consider doing the same.

CHRIS CARLSON

PART 3

SPEAKING

Speaking

Speaking should be a critical component of your prospecting plan. Speaking in front of people who comprise your ideal prospects is the easiest and fastest way to fill your pipeline with highly-qualified, highly-motivated prospects. Think about it. You are in front of a group of people, maybe it is a small group of 4-5 people or maybe it is a large group of over 100 people. They are there for a reason. They key now is to establish your credibility and take the first step in developing a relationship with these potential prospects.

Unfortunately, far too many salespeople make one or both of the following mistakes.

Mistake Number One is making the talk more of a commercial than a presentation/discussion of ideas, problems or issues. Nothing turns an audience off faster than when the speaker tries to disguise presentation as a commercial.

Mistake Number Two is when the speaker approaches the talk through his/her viewpoint instead of through the viewpoint of the audience. Face it, the audience wants it to be about them. Their problems, their issues, their needs, their opportunities. Even during a presentation, your audience is tuning in to their favorite radio station, WIIFM (What's In It For Me). You must give them what they want.

This is not a book about public speaking, so I am not going to talk about structure or style of your presentations. But, I do want to encourage you to do three things with your audience.

First, get them engaged. You want your presentation to be more of a conversation than a lecture. Your audience does not want to be talked down to, but rather wants to participate in the "conversation."

Second, add value. Your presentation should provide so much value to your audience that they cannot wait to get more from you. If you add tremendous value in your presentation and then make an offer to give them even more value, you will be amazed at the response. Examples would be to give away a free report, an e-book, a coupon or even a copy of your book. These types of resources allow you to continue your "conversation" with your audience.

Third, get their contact information. In return for the free report, e-book, coupon or book, *ask* for their contact information. You may ask for their e-mail address, physical address or both. Once you capture their contact information, you are now in a position to put them into an on-going marketing campaign. A campaign that allows you to continue to add value and establish credibility. Remember, most people are not "right now" buyers, so you want to continue the conversation with them all the way through their Buy Line. When they do get ready to buy, you will be top of mind.

So, if you agree with the notion that speaking should be a critical component of your prospecting plan, you are probably thinking to yourself, "OK Chris, I buy into the concept, but how do I get speaking gigs?" Let's answer that question right now.

Now, there are two ways to speak in front of your targeted audience. You can fill the seats or have somebody else fill the seats. I can tell you from experience that it is much easier to have somebody else fill the seats. The best way to do that is to be invited to speak at an event that is already scheduled.

I don't know if you have had the opportunity like I have to be a program chair for an organization. If you have, you know how challenging it can be to find quality speakers to fill up all of your meeting slots. Anytime a speaker is dropped into your lap, you have had a great day. The system I am going to talk about will make you a hero to many of these program chairs. With a little time, effort and money, you can secure several speaking gigs in the next 90 days.

Here is a 6-step process to help you get speaking engagements.

Step 1: Determine Which Organizations To Which You Want To Speak

This may seem obvious, but the fact is, not all organizations are created equal. If you are going to invest your time, effort and money into speaking, then it is critical that you are speaking to the right groups. So let's give some thought as to what may be the right groups for you. You need to consider things like:

Location. Are they local, regional or national?

Type. Are they industry based, community based or mission based?

Size. Do they need to be a certain size that would produce enough of an audience to make it worth your while?

Paid vs. Non-Paid. While it is always nice to get paid, my advice is to not focus on the fee because the money you can eventually make from future clients in the audience will far surpass any speaker's fee you will be paid.

The bottom line is that you need to focus on organizations that you can best serve. Remember, more is not better. Better is better.

Step 2: Determine Points of Contacts

Now that you have a list of organizations to which you would like to speak, your next step is to do some research to find out the names and addresses of the Points of Contacts in these organizations. The easiest way to do this to go to their website. Look around to see if they have a program chair. If one is not listed, just find out the name of the Executive Director. While you are on the site, find out the mailing address of the organization. You can now start a spreadsheet that will have the name of the organization, the Point of Contact and the mailing address. It doesn't matter if this list contains 5 names, 55 names or 555 names, what you do next is exactly the same.

Step 3: Create A Marketing Campaign

Your next step is to create a marketing campaign to these organizations. Your goal of this campaign is to get people to contact you and eventually invite you to speak to their organization. Please keep the following in mind. If you believe that speaking can help your prospecting efforts, this is not a one and done campaign. It is a campaign that you can use for months and even years.

Step 4: Create Titles For Your Talks

Next, you need to come up with titles for at least three talks.   The reason you need multiple titles is that it increases your chances to have a talk that interests your Point of Contact. Also, make sure your title is not boring. Make it have some pizzazz. For example, if the title of your talk is Retirement Planning, you will not create much interest.   But if the title of your talk is "The 5 Biggest Mistakes People Make That Cost Them Millions of Dollars In Retirement," you will create much more interest. Caveat. You still have to deliver great value in your talk. It can't just be a captivating title with crappy content.

Step 5: Create And Mail 4 Post Cards

Now that you have the titles of your talk, you need to create your first postcard that you are going to mail to your Points of Contact. This post card will simply say who you are, the title of your three talks and how they can get a hold of you. If you so desire, you can give them the URL of your website. This post card peaks their interest.

In 3 to 4 weeks, you are going to send out your second postcard that goes into detail about one of your talks. Tell the Point of Contact what their members will get out of the talk.   If you have something to offer you might point out that each attendee will receive a copy of my book, "Spend Your Retirement Years In Your Dream House, Not The Poor House."   Again, let them know how they can get a hold of you.

The 3rd and 4th postcards follow the same pattern. Give the details of one of your talks and what their members will get out of the talk. Again, there should be 3 to 4 weeks between post cards.

As an FYI, the thriftiest way to do this sequence is to (1) use a service like Vista Print to print your post cards, (2) create labels from your excel spreadsheet and (3) buy stamps from the post office. You will spend less than 50 cents per post card to include printing and mailing. There are also services that can everything for you to include printing, labeling, postage and mailing. It obviously cost more, but it does free up a lot of your time.

Step 6: Follow Up With Organizations

When you send out your series of post cards, you **will** have people contact you. But keep in mind, the majority will not. So if you are truly committed to expanding your speaking opportunities, you need to follow up with the Points of Contact. Whether you choose to do this via e-mail or via phone, you will pick up additional opportunities with this activity. The good news is that when you reach out to them, they have received 4 pieces of correspondence from you. The conversation will go much smoother and it will allow you to determine if there are opportunities to speak with this particular organization, either in the short term or the long term.

Follow Up With Attendees

Once you have secured a speaking engagement, make sure you have a system to follow up with attendees. Don't make the mistake of not gathering the contact information of those in attendance. After all, these people probably belong to your target market. There are two basic ways to collect this information.

The first way is to ask the organization for list of people, along with their contact information. Many will provide this with no problem.

The second way is to collect the information during your talk. An example would be to offer a free report and/or a copy of your slides if they text their e-mail address to a phone number that is attached to an auto responder.

By having the attendees' contact information, you can put them into your normal, on-going marketing campaign.

Once you go through the campaign the first time, create a second campaign to the same list. You can create new titles or just send the same 4 post cards you did in your initial campaign. This system *will* result in speaking opportunities.

I realize that not everyone likes the idea of speaking to groups. But this is what I know. If you commit to marketing yourself as a speaker to organizations and then stick with it, it will result in you attracting prospects into your pipeline. Sometimes it happens on the first very talk, other times it takes a few talks. But what would you rather do, make cold calls or speak to groups of potential prospects?

PART 4

REFERRALS

Referrals

In my opinion, there is no better way to position yourself with a prospect than to receive a kick-ass referral. By default, you are already above the line of credibility when your referral source says great things about you and suggests to a person that they should meet with you. I bet if you asked most salespeople their most effective prospecting method, they would probably respond with, "referrals."

Yet, if this is the most effective prospecting method, and the best way for salespeople to position themselves, why do so few salespeople excel at this activity? My belief is that most salespeople do not have a strategy or a system to continually ask for and receive referrals. For you to take advantage of the tremendous opportunities created from referrals, you need to have a R.A.P., a Referral Action Program. Let's take a look at 5 key components of a R.A.P.:

- ➢ Setting Goals
- ➢ Identify Centers of Influence
- ➢ Weekly Planning
- ➢ Research on Centers of Influence
- ➢ Way To Prompt The Introduction

GOALS

The single biggest reason salespeople fail to receive the number of referrals they want is that they do not have a goal. I do a ton of training workshops and I always ask each group the question, "who has a goal for the number of referrals you want to receive each week?" Of all the groups I ask this of, I would say less than 2% of the participants have such a goal. As the saying goes, "if you don't know what you are shooting for, it is pretty hard to hit it."

I believe you **must** have a goal for the number of referrals you want each week. I cannot tell you what that goal should be, but you need to establish one and be committed to it.

Too often, salespeople just pick a number out of the air and say to themselves, "I want 5 referrals each week." Most times they have no idea why they picked that number other than it sounded good.

Instead of guessing, my advice is to review your activity matrix (you do have one don't you?) to determine what that weekly number should be. By activity matrix I mean your success ratio in terms of:

- ➤ Calls-to-Appointments
- ➤ Appointments-to-Opportunities
- ➤ Opportunities-to-Presentations
- ➤ Presentations-to-Closed Deals

By working backwards, you can determine this ratio with remarkable accuracy. Once you have determined what you believe your weekly referral goal should be, be committed. Remember, it is a **goal**, not a "nice to have."

If you struggle with getting a consistent amount of referrals, I suggest that you set a small goal, say one per week, then you can increase it when you consistently hit this number each and every week.

I realize that not everyone depends solely on referrals for first time appointments, so you may be doing other prospecting activities to help you hit your revenue goals. But, the objective in your Referral Action Program is for you to develop a 100% referral based business.

IDENTIFY CENTERS OF INFLUENCE

To achieve your goal of a 100% referral based business, you need to have Centers of Influence (COIs) who are continually introducing you to prospects. Identifying COIs is something that most salespeople do not spend enough time on. Too often I hear salespeople say, "I am working with a couple of CPAs and a couple of Attorneys to try and get referrals from them."

You need to be much more thoughtful and strategic than that. You need to understand that all of your competitors are going after CPAs and attorneys. If you want to have them as good COIs you need to differentiate yourself from your competitors. Make sure you add value to these COIs before you ask for a referral or introduction.

Give some thought as to whom else besides CPAs and attorneys could be great COIs. Who else sells, or is connected to, the types of prospects you want to meet? For example, if your target market is manufacturing companies, do know the bankers or equipment salespeople that are calling on these types of companies? These type of people can be great COIs. Identify these type of potential COIs and reach out to them to see if you can establish a mutually beneficial relationship.

Your best COIs should be your current clients. This is obvious to some, but unfortunately most salespeople do not tap into this phenomenal resource. I cannot tell you how many salespeople have made comments to me like, "I don't want to push them for a referral, or, I don't want to appear needy." Are you kidding me? These are people that are the beneficiaries of that salesperson's great work and yet they don't feel confident to ask for an introduction? When you take a look at your clients, which of your current clients cast a wide net and are influential in your target market?

Now let's become a little more focused on actual names. I believe that there are two types of COIs. First are those COIs that you already have a great relationship with and are currently referring you. The second type is what I call Developing COIs. Those are people with whom you have a relationship, but the relationship has not yet developed to the point that they are giving you referrals.

Take some time to start listing names. My experience tells me that you can probably list between 3-10 names of Current COIs.

My experience also tells me that you can list between 25 and 50 names of COIs that need to be developed. Once you have names on this list, you need to start reaching out to them to determine if over time you can move them onto the Current COI list.

OK, you have some ideas and some names, now what?

As you know, developing relationships with prospects takes time. This is also true with COIs. Don't expect to meet a COI for the first time and think they are going to open up their contact list to you.

Don't push, because you push the COI away. Many of them are being pursued by your competitors and these COIs are evaluating you to see how you are different and, if in fact, you could add value to the people they know.

Look to add value to your potential COI's business or personal life. It could be as simple as recommending a book or it could be that you send them some business. What you do is not as important as actually doing something. Over time, always look for ways to add value, both big and small.

Understand that some potential COIs will become good or great COIs and some won't. That is why it is important to continually reach out and meet with potential COIs. It is just like prospecting, you always have to be filling the pipeline.

Whatever you do, do not give up. There will be times that you are on fire and there will be dry spells. Many salespeople get discouraged during the dry spells and abandon their Referral Action Program. They go back to cold calling or networking or some other ineffective prospecting method. Don't let this happen to you. Stay the course.

Let's face it. Developing COIs is not a fast process. It takes time, effort and patience. But if you are committed to the process, the pay-off is enormous.

WEEKLY PLANNING

Many salespeople think that getting a consistent level of referrals will require a huge investment of time. They often say to me, "Chris, I am already working long hours. How am I going to find the time to meet with people to get referrals?"

It will not take you much time each week if you have a Referral Action Program. What you do need to do is set aside time each week to plan for your success. In reality, just a few minutes of planning each week can put you on the path to getting both the quantity and quality of referrals you want.

Here are the key steps you need to take each and very week:

As you plan each week, look at your calendar.

➢ Take a look at the people you are already scheduled to meet or call. Maybe you need to take a look at the association meetings you plan to attend to determine if you will be seeing clients or COIs.

➢ Write down the names of the people you will see or talk to. These will be the people from whom you will ask for referrals this week. They could be COIs, they could be friends or they could be current clients. The key is to have a list of names as a reminder to ASK.

➢ Sometimes your calendar may not be full, so refer back to the COI lists you created. Pay special attention to those you are trying to develop. Maybe you will be in his/her area and can drop in. Maybe you could send a quick e-mail inviting them for a cup of coffee. So instead of being in the office doing non-productive busywork, you can make it productive time in developing and deepening relationships with current and future sources of referrals.

➢ Now that you have a list of names, send a quick e-mail telling them that you would like their help. The e-mail may sound like this: "Bill, during our meeting on Thursday, I would like to take 5 minutes and ask you to help me brainstorm a marketing idea I am putting together. I know you will have some great ideas."

> During you meeting, you must be committed to having the referral conversation. Don't wait to the end of the meeting and try to rush the process and say something like, "Bill do you know anybody you could refer me to?" Instead say something like, "Bill, as I mentioned in my e-mail earlier in the week, I would like your help in brainstorming a marketing idea I am putting together. What I have decided to do is build a 100% referral based business. What I mean by that is that I am only going to take on new clients if they are referred to me by a current client or professional partner like you. What do you think of that concept?"

Now out of role-play. They will always say it is a good idea, or some variation of that. Now you will be able to transition into discussing specific people with Bill that he can introduce you to. We will talk more about the exact language of that conversation shortly.

There is a very important point I must address here. Many salespeople feel very uncomfortable asking for help like this. I have heard on many occasions comments like, "I don't want to appear desperate or needy." My coaching advice is to get over it. People want to help you, so make it easy for them to do so. Asking for help in developing a 100% referral based business is not needy. It is a phenomenal business strategy. Your mindset is really the key to success in creating your R.A.P.

Too often I talk with salespeople who come to the end of the week and they have not asked for referrals. They did not plan to fail, they just failed to plan. Don't let this happen to you.

Now think about what we have discussed so far. Not only have we established a weekly goal for referrals, but we have just created a simple system to make it easy to accomplish that goal each week. And the key to success in this system is that we did not create so much extra work that you get discouraged and quit the process.

RESEARCH ON CENTERS OF INFLUENCE

You have now identified whom you are going to talk to this week regarding referrals. You cannot just meet with a COI and ask, "who do you know that you could refer me to?" That question is almost always answered with, "I can't think of anybody right now, but when I do, I will let you know." The problem is that they rarely do. Not because they are bad people, they just get busy and forget about the conversation. So what we want to do is avoid the zero, as in you get zero referrals from this conversation.

By doing some research, you can come up with the names of people that your COI may know and then you can ask for introductions to specific people. By going to some of the sources we will discuss, you can always come up with people that would be ideal prospects for you.

Where can you look in your research efforts? There are many sources, but here are a few that I have found to be invaluable in coming up with names of whom my COIs know.

LinkedIn is a great source to find out who your COI is connected to. Browsing through their connections will always produce names you can discuss.

You can Google your COI to find out more information about them. This will often provide more ideas of where you can look to find out whom they may know.

Facebook is becoming a much more popular business tool. Many of your COIs may have a business Facebook page and you can gather great insight and information from that page.

You can research the website of your COI. You will be able to discover such things as whom he/she works with, key customers, key partners, charities they support and possible associations they may belong to.

You might use a tool like First Research or Dun and Bradstreet to find out additional data about the company.

And finally, if you know your COI serves on any Boards, you might look at that organization's web site to see whom his or her fellow board members might be. Are any of these fellow board members people you would like to be introduced to?

There are certainly other tools you can use to determine whom your COI might know, but these are great places to start. Remember, the reason you are doing this research is to be able to provide your COI specific people that you would like to be introduced to.

Now that you have done the research and have some names, right down those names on a 3x5 card that you can use in your meeting with your COI. Right down 2-4 names for every meeting. If you write down too many names, your COI will zone out on you. You will then take this 3x5 card with you to your meeting and ask questions about the specific names on the card. We will give you a couple of examples of those questions in the next section.

So buy a couple of packs of 3x5 cards. It might be one of the best investments you will ever make.

WAYS TO PROMPT THE INTRODUCTION

This is one of the most important steps in your R.A.P. because you can quickly go from getting no names when you ask a COI for a referral, to being introduced to 2, 3 or even 4 prospects every time you meet with that COI.

Let me ask if this has ever happened to you. You have a great meeting with a COI. Everything is moving in the right direction and you feel confident that they will gladly introduce you to potential prospects. The moment of truth comes and you ask something like, "who do you know that could use my services?" You can't wait to start writing down some names when you get a response that sounds like, "I can't think of anybody right now, but when I do, I will give you a call."

Talk about the air going out of the balloon! That "feel good moment" just turned into a "feel like crap moment." What makes it worse is that they never call back. They never call back not because they are bad people, they just get busy with other priorities.

You have probably heard the saying, "if you don't like the answers, change the questions." Well, our problem is that we asked them the wrong question. The wrong question leads to no results. So, what we need to do is to change the question. Asking the right question will get us great results. So what are the right questions? Let me give you a couple of examples.

One question you can ask goes like this, "Dave, I was reviewing some of your LinkedIn connections and a couple of people caught my eye. Take a look at this 3x5 card. Knowing what you know about the people on this card and knowing what you know about me, which ones would it make sense for you to introduce me to?" Now instead of getting the dreaded response, "I can't think of anybody right now," you will begin discussing the names on the 3x5 card. You can ask for some more information on the ones he feels might be a good fit.

A second question you can ask goes like this, "Dave, there are some people in your Vistage Group that are on my list of targeted prospects. Take a look at the names on this 3x5 card. Knowing what you know about me and knowing what you know about them, which ones do you think I should target?"

There are certainly several ways you can ask this question, but the key is to give them some specific names you can discuss so they just don't shut down on you.

Once you have the discussion regarding who they think would be a good fit, ask the following question. "Dave, what is the best way for me to be introduced to them?" Now Dave is thinking about how he can help you. You can give your COI the 3 x 5 Card at the end of your meeting as a reminder of what they are going to do on your behalf. It becomes their homework. You will be amazed that they will not throw it away until they fulfil their commitment to get you an introduction.

Imagine the impact on your business when you implement the 3x5 card approach and you go from getting no names to 2-4 names every time you meet with a COI. It will change your business forever.

So, in review, we have talked about 5 key components of a R.A.P.:

> Setting Goals
> Identify Centers of Influence
> Weekly Planning
> Research on Centers of Influence
> Way To Prompt The Introduction

The key part of a Referral Action Program is **Action**! Here is what I know. If you take some of the time your are currently spending on ineffective prospecting methods and invest it in your R.A.P., your pipeline will be full of great prospects and before your know it, you will never have to cold call again.

CHRIS CARLSON

PART 5

THE EXPERTS

The Experts

I submit that all of the methods outlined in this book will help you fill your pipeline with highly-qualified, highly-motivated prospects. I have experienced it in my own business, but I think it is important that you hear more than just my opinion. I have seen others achieve tremendous success using these methods and I want you to hear their stories.

I want to introduce you to eight individuals that I consider experts in prospecting. Each one of these individuals has a unique talent and a unique methodology in filling their sales pipeline.

John Cote

John Cote is the CEO of John Cote & Associates, a consulting firm he founded to create growth strategies, story-based marketing campaigns and customer engagement systems for businesses and organizations of any size. John is the award winning author of multiple Amazon.com #1 Best Selling books including, ***Healthcare Elsewhere - What You Can Learn From These 21 People Who Got Their Medical Care Abroad That Will Save You Money, Time and Quite Possibly Your Life*** and ***Mobilize Your Customers - Create Powerful Word of Mouth Advertising Using Social Media, Video and Mobile Marketing to Attract New Customers and Skyrocket Your Profits.***

John is also the creator and host of Healthcare Elsewhere, the world's leading medical tourism podcast. As a patient advocate and educator, he interviews patients who share their inspiring success stories. He also interviews leading doctors and healthcare experts worldwide.

Chris: John, I really want to thank you for taking time out of your busy schedule to visit with me today.

John: Hey, it's my pleasure Chris.

Chris: Well John to get started, can you give us a brief background of John Cote?

John: After college I had joined the military and became a pilot, a jet pilot in a marine corps and then that transitioned over into an airline career. I thought everything was great with that until 9/11 happened, that was a while back. All of a sudden I realized, "Hey, my company could go out of

87

business. I could be on the street and needing to be doing something else because nobody else would be hiring a pilot at that point," obviously because everybody was hurting in the industry. Over time we started looking at different alternatives of what we might do to, you know when I say we, I mean my wife and I and our family and everything, and one of the things that we looked at was marketing.

We got into having a marketing agency as a way to help other companies with their problems, getting found and things like this and this was back in a time when Facebook was a new thing. Facebook fan pages were new. We were doing a lot of social media marketing and I'd help some friends with their companies and that led to other clients.

The next thing we know, we were up and running. After a while, that started getting commoditized, a lot people were offering that very inexpensively. Fiverr came in to being and people started outsourcing a lot of that very inexpensively. We decided to pivot in a different direction and look more towards, instead of doing things for people, showing them how to do it on the consulting aspect of it and using books and podcasts and other digital content video and things like that to help promote their business.

Chris: Awesome. Why don't you tell us a little bit about your current business model.

John: Sure. What we do, my company is called John Cote and Associates. One of the primary things that we do is use digital outreach to basically help people get their company found in their niche. We've done everything from plastic surgery centers to cosmetic dentistry, international medical tourism destinations, local small companies, like restaurants and things like that. Really any kind of business out there that we would come across. Then we ended up getting into this medical tourism niche through happenstance, actually, I can get into the story, if you're interested, but that's pretty much what we're doing right now.

Chris: I mean, the podcasting thing is so fascinating to me. Why don't you give us a brief description of the podcast, Healthcare Elsewhere.

John: Healthcare Elsewhere is an interview-based show where we talk with some of the medical professionals around the world and most specifically patients, people who have actually travelled to another country or another part of their country to get a specific medical treatment that they couldn't get where they were because it was either too expensive or in the case of stem cell therapies, it may not be available because it hasn't been approved by that local government's medical board and things like that.

Long story short, I had a book out called, *__Mobilize Your Customers__*. Four years ago or something like that, one of the people who was in charge of putting on this huge medical tourism conference had like 2,000 attendees from 80 countries, was looking for a word-of-mouth advertising speaker. She typed in "word of mouth advertising speaker," into Google and a lot of those key words were in the subtitle of my book. My link popped up on Amazon for that book, so they bought the book, read it, loved it, and said, "Hey, we'd love for you to come out and speak at this conference." I was like, "Great! Happy to do it. What's medical tourism?"

They kind of explained it to me and I went and did a bunch of research and put together a custom presentation. In the process of doing that, I talked with everyone in the speech about how podcasting was really blowing up. This was about two years ago and how they really needed to take a look at using that as a way to help connect with potential clients, right? They are very high-value clients and patients. Everyone thought that was a great idea, but nobody ended up doing anything with it. After a couple of months went by, I went on Amazon and on iTunes and did a search again, and nothing came up. I said, "All right, let's go ahead," and I got my team and we decided to do our own.

Chris: So basically from the time that you made the suggestion to the time that you said, "Hey, let's do our own," that was a couple-month process?

John: Yeah, I think we did the speaking engagement in November, or something like that, a couple of years ago, and then, after the holidays, I kind of noticed nothing was happening and about the end of January I said, "All right, let's go ahead and do our own." We set a goal, 10 weeks, we wanted to launch. I had three goals: I wanted to launch in 10 weeks, I wanted it to be a world class interview type show, because I'm not a medical tourism expert or a doctor, so I wanted to be able to bring other people who were experts and who had experienced these things, and to be able to provide content that would be hugely helpful to people who were somewhere on their journey who just didn't know where else to turn and what to do.

We were able to do that and so we launched in April of 2014. Then we did it with the intent of taking the content, some of the recordings that we had done and turning them into a book as well, which also came out like 4 or 5 months later. We turned it into a best seller on Amazon.

Chris: You know, John, you really are my hero, because we talk about prospecting through positioning and you have done two of the things that I think are so critical for people today, is not only the book, but also the podcast. You've done both, so congratulations for your success on both of those.

John: Well thanks, I appreciate it.

Chris: Let's go back in time. You talked with your team, "Let's launch this podcast." What were some of the milestones, the hurdles, or the things that you had to either research or do, to go from zero to launching that podcast?

John: I set a goal of 10 weeks and that was probably pretty ridiculous because we wanted something that was going to be fairly high value content. I could have just gone out and literally, just do like I did with my first book, I turned on my iPhone voice recorder and started recording my book and we got it transcribed and turned into my book. We could have hooked up an external microphone to my iPhone and started recording and just doing interviews that way. But I wanted to do some fairly high production value, but more bang for the buck. I didn't want to spend a whole zillion dollars, so we already had, at the time, we were still working out of my house. I had no real need to have an office or anything like that. We had a big basement that was finished that had plenty of area for a studio to set up. We were doing a daily show to start with. We were doing 4 or 5 interviews a day for a couple of weeks and then more after that.

It got to the point where, eventually, we did end up getting some office space, because I needed a place that I could do it quietly, cause it wasn't fair to my wife and kids to say, "Hey, I need you to be quiet all day while I'm trying to record this thing." The dogs were running around and everything else. You don't have to do that, you can certainly go out and figure out what you need to do, but we bought about $1,000 worth of equipment; a microphone and pre-amplifier and things like that. I already had the computers, we already had a full video studio, green screen and all that capability.

Then I bought a course, John Lee Dumas' course, Podcasters Paradise to learn how to podcast, how to interview someone, how to go through the technical process. Went through the modules that I needed to learn what we needed and started doing interviews within a couple of weeks. That was probably the hardest part. Not just finding good people to interview, but also tracking them down and setting up systems so that, "Oh well, I can't do it this time." Or "I'm over in India and we're on the other side of the world and the time difference." And everything else.

It took some time to get all that figured out, but once we got our systems in place, it came together and we were able to get, I think, about 35 interviews done before we actually launched. I already had those in the can and ready to go.

Chris: That is awesome. What you just said is, I think, very, very critical. What was the best method that you used to actually get somebody to agree to be a guest on your show?

John: That's one of the beautiful things about this model, I think, is that, for example, I had a list of people that had seen me speak. Because when I'm on stage, I always do a crowd-grabber type of a campaign, where instead of saying, "Hey, give me your business cards and I'll give you a chance to win a free book," we gave away copies of my book. I brought 200 copies of the book and just gave it away to people, but then there was also a sheet on there where they could text their name and e-mail to a specific number and get, basically, an audio recording of what I had just done, plus a copy of my slides. It was a really good thing to give away, that people were interested in.

We built a list of, I don't know, probably about 150 or so people and then I headed to the show room floor at the Trade Show, it was at Caesar's Palace in Las Vegas, and there's thousands of people milling about. We were just handing out books and signing autographs and having a good time. I built my list that way and so I just reached out to those people and said, "Hey, you might remember me talking about this and if you didn't, here's the thing." So, I showed them and gave them some authority piece, basically, my speech. They got to hear it and see the slides. "We would love to interview you for the show, here's the concept we were talking about, this is what it's going to look like."

I had come up with the sheet of information that I needed that basically had, "Hey, this is how you'll do it, this is what the questions we'll ask, it's a half an hour show, this is how much time I need of yours." We just started saying that and for most people, when we reached out to them, initially, almost without fail they would say, "they loved it" because you're giving them something of great value to them. Even if hardly anybody hears the actual podcast itself, they have the ability to embed it and have a third party interview on their website to kind of show people that, "Hey, they're legit," or to give them more authority and everything else. It was a great way to break the ice and make connections with people and get them to come in and do the interview and then for some of those people, they eventually became clients of mine.

Chris: That is awesome. That initial outreach was typically via e-mail?

John: Yeah that's right. For some of them that I had already made a connection with and talked with personally, if I had their cell phone, I would just call them flat out, or I'd have my assistant call them and say, "Hey, we met, you remember?" "Oh yeah, what's going on?" "Hey, we're doing this show and we'd love to interview you. What's your schedule looking like? I'll have my assistant set up something for you or whatever."

Again, you don't have to have an assistant do that. You can set up ScheduleOnce or similar program like that, which we use now, to handle a lot of that stuff. We just send them the link and they pick a time that works for them. I think, because of the level of people that we were trying to approach, by reaching out to them personally, that's one thing, but having my assistant call them, just kind of, "Oh, my assistant will call your assistant," kind of a thing with some of the higher end people we were trying to reach. I don't know, it just seemed to give a little bit more credence to, "Oh, this a legit thing, it wasn't just something we were just making up on the fly," which we weren't. We had a good plan in place and we told them that we were just starting the production, the things were going to be airing here in about 4-6 more weeks. Then we would contact them and let them know when it was going.

We rarely have had any problems with anyone saying, "No." I think maybe I've had two doctors who just flat out said, "Nah, not interested." They were concerned about whatever, liability or whatever, and they just didn't want to do it. I'm like, "All right, that's fine."

Chris: That's two out of dozens? Hundreds?

John: Yeah, dozens. We've had over 110 episodes or something and we actually kind of broke the podcasting rule. I took some time off, took a hiatus, kind of for the summer and that turned into the fall. We've got another 20 or so episodes in the can, ready to go. We're just about to start off the second season here.

We've kind of run it almost more like on a TV production schedule, where there's kind of an off-season, but I mean, if people are looking for it, there's plenty of episodes. There's 100+ episodes that they can listen to. Interestingly enough, not too long after our interview, I have a meeting with Hollywood producers who contacted me about doing a TV show. They actually have listened to almost every single one of our episodes and they love the show, they love the concept. They want to make a reality TV show about it, about the good side, not the gotcha side of it, but how people have a problem or an issue medically and they can't get it done in their country or they can't afford it and they're traveling to another country to get it done.

There's some compelling stories there. I'm biased, of course. I've been telling these stories and helping patients tell these stories for the last year and a half now and it's been a lot of fun. We've had just some unbelievable moments on the show and so now all of a sudden we're looking at perhaps being involved, in some way, in a reality TV show.

Chris: Obviously the podcast is having a huge impact on your business then?

John: Oh yeah, absolutely. As a matter of fact, one of the things they were looking for help with was perhaps getting introductions to companies that are doing this and patients. Since I already have kind of a steady feed of this, they were looking for something in particular. I said, "Okay." I definitely have a couple of companies in mind that I can hook them up with that have already indicated that they're interested, but that notwithstanding, some of these companies just came to me recently, they saw the show or heard my show, heard about it somehow or another, stumbled across it online, or whatever. I've had more than a few companies reach out and say, "Hey, I'm with the marketing department or I'm the CEO or I'm the head doctor, and we would love to be on your show. We like what you're doing. Would you consider us?" I'll vet them out and check them out and see who they're all about and what their message is. Then we'll do an interview with them. Now I have people starting to come to me. Seeking me out to be on my show.

Chris: What have been the biggest surprises, either good or bad, about doing a podcast?

John: Don't do a daily show! I started out that way. I got to know John Dumas a little bit, he's a great guy and he and Kate have been very open with their time with us and we did some extra things for Podcasters Paradise and kind of put out some of the information about what we were doing and what was working for us. They've been just very awesome and supportive. I can't even put myself even close to the same league as what he's doing, the kind of revenue they're pulling in and the numbers they're doing, the downloads and everything. They're doing a spectacular job.

If you're not familiar with John Lee Dumas, he's kind of the king of podcasting right now with Entrepreneur On Fire. He started off doing a daily show. Everyone told him, "Don't do that! That's crazy. No one wants to hear you every day." But it works well for his niche and for us, we didn't think that we were interested in doing a daily show and doing 365 shows in a year, not that there wasn't enough content, but I didn't because I also have a company I have to run, right?

We wanted to do it for a couple of months so I'd have enough content so that we could create a book that would be ready for me to speak at the next year's medical tourism conference, which then lead to me getting more clients. It was important for me to do that, initially, so we had a ton of content that we could sift through and figure out which are going to be the best ones for the book.

It's not particularly difficult, podcasting, but when you start trying to do it every single day, just the sheer volume of trying to set up all those interviews and then people cancel and they can't make it or the flake out, their microphone's not working today all the little things that happen, you got to reschedule, all of a sudden that snowballs. Then I can't stress enough, whenever you are getting ready to go, let's say you're going to do a weekly show, right? Something like that, I think that's a good starting goal for people, 50 episodes a year. Go out and get, maybe, I don't know, 15 or 20 episodes done.

Our first published episode, Episode 1, was actually like the 19th or 20th one that we did. I didn't do them chronologically, there was no need for me to do that, none of them were time-topical or anything. What we did was we took the best of the 35 interviews, from a story perspective, about a woman who had multiple sclerosis, and went down to Panama to get therapies done, stem cell therapies, that allowed her to not be in a wheelchair. That was extremely compelling and it was probably the most impressive story that we had. It also gave me time to get better at being an interviewer and a podcaster, because I didn't know anything about podcasting at the time.

Chris: How else are you using the podcast in your marketing efforts?

John: I mean, for us, I get a lot of requests for interviews on how would we use the podcast in marketing and things like that. We are consulting with people, sometimes, mostly the medical field who are looking at how do we reach out and find more people in our niche that we're trying to reach, that's different than the way most other surgeons are kind of word of mouth or whatever.

For example, if you're into knee replacement or hip replacement or knee surgeries for athletes. That's an extremely competitive field, it's also extremely lucrative. Some of the best doctors run big, huge practices, they're making millions of dollars, tens of millions of dollars in fees every year for that kind of stuff. They're constantly looking for new people, new patients, to bring in. They're very competitive. Having something like this where you would maybe have interviews with sports stars or other maybe semi-professional or NCAA athletes who have gone through and get a better idea of what they're doing for them and how their helping them.

So we're helping with consulting on those kinds of things and that's been interesting. On the medical tourism aspect of it, I love making the connections with people. Sometimes we're able to help patients find people call and say, "Well, where can I find ...?" I'm like, "I don't know. I need to talk to a medical tourism facilitator," but I can suggest people to them. Say, "Hey, if you're looking to go to this country, talk to these people or that country, try these couple of companies," which is nice.

By doing all of that and basically providing value to people in the community, both from the patient perspective and the business perspective, the more value we provide, the more people tend to find us and want to do business with us. I learned that from some of my mentors and from John Dumas. John Lee Dumas talks about this specifically, when he really started making money was when he figured out that he needed to stop trying to get things from people and instead provide value for them as much as possible. After doing his podcast for about 6 months to a year, he actually finally started monetizing it. No one should go into it thinking, "Oh, I'm going to start this podcast and in two weeks I'm going to have a bunch of people paying me $100,000 a year." You've got to build an audience. It takes time, it's not something that you're just going to go out and do a get-rich-quick or anything like that.

Chris: I think that's important advice. One of the things I do want to compliment you on is you went from, as you said earlier, knowing nothing about medical tourism to now, you are probably the recognized expert and the go-to person for people to make connections with.

John: Well, yeah, I mean, I like to be a connector and connect people like that. I would hardly consider myself an expert. There's people who are medical professionals who know a lot more about this than I do. I just have a show, I have a voice. I have the ability to bring these people on. I'm always looking for people who are way more knowledgeable than me to bring them on the show to provide great content for people. Great information so that they can make informed decisions.

I always tell everyone, "Hey, look, I'm not a medical professional. I don't know all the answers, but I can tell you that you should maybe listen to a show or two on something that's interesting to you and then go out and do the research and figure it out. Do your background checks and everything else." It's not like we're going out like the FDA or something like that and doing background checks on all these companies. We vet them out and make sure that they're legit and that they've actually had patients and things like this. Sometimes we've had start-up companies.

For me, it's really about how can we best serve the patients. How can we give them the content that they need and the information that they need. In the process of doing that, we're also serving the business owners, who then become my clients.

Chris: That's a great model. Emerson says, "If you want more, give more."

John: Yeah, absolutely. We're certainly not the first ones to come up with that, we're just copying others who have done it before us and it's working well.

Chris: Well John, what advice would you give to someone who's considering launching their own podcast?

John: I would say figure out, what's your message and who are you talking to? John Lee Dumas talks about this famously, and others do as well, who's your avatar? When you think you have it, niche it down, niche down more. I mean, like a medical tourism podcast, that's pretty niche. I mean, but I could niche it down even more if I wanted to. I could do one that's only about medical tourism for, say, knee and hip replacements and medical tourism only for stem cell therapies or things like that. Try and go as narrow as you can, because that's, in my opinion, where the dollars are. We're starting to get more and more clients out of the medical tourism arena.

We're also getting other clients that happen to come to us from a variety of other things that we're doing speaking engagements or books or whatever we get referred. We're happy to do business with them in different areas, but we're getting into this medical tourism aspect because, as an example, the second year that I spoke, I was very well prepared, had a much better idea, we talked about using podcasting and digital content to attract an audience and everything. What that did was it attracted the CEO of a large organization that's building a huge medical tourism city, essentially, down in Central America, that's about to be announced. We basically were invited, my wife and I, to go fly down there to this location at their expense, to go check it all out. They wanted us to help with their digital outreach, eventually. So we've been doing a bunch of work with them and now we actually have a seat on their board because of the work that we've done with them. All of that started because of the podcast and because I was willing to go out and start interviewing people in a niche that I didn't know anything about.

I guess, the long answer to your short question is, if you're looking at doing a podcast, figure out how are you serving the people that are going to be listening. If you're thinking that, "Well, I'm just going to give some marketing tips and hope that people are going to buy my show, buy advertising on my show or buy my product." That's a great place to be eventually, but you've got to give them stuff first. Really good, solid definable content. Figure out who your niche is, what is it that they need, what's their pain point, and what is their problem, and how can you help them solve that. Build your user-base and your following and as you do that and grow and realize it's not going to happen over night. It's going to take some time. Then once you get that going, then you can start asking them for things back, like, "Hey, buy my course." Or "Here's an interesting book that we wrote." Or whatever.

Chris: John, let me ask you this before we get out of here today. There's probably some people saying, "Man, that's the marketing guru that I need to talk to." What's the best way for people to get in contact with you?

John: They can contact me at john@johncote.net. I'm all over LinkedIn and I'm on Instagram and Facebook and all these other kind of places. You can always Facebook message me as well. If I don't see it, my assistant usually picks that up and let's me know, "Hey, you've got a message coming in about such and such," but happy to talk with people about what they're doing and how that applies to their business and how they can use digital content to increase their revenue.

Chris: John, thanks so much for your time today.

John: Oh, it's been my pleasure. I really appreciate you having me on today, Chris.

John's website is www.johncote.net.

Mario Fachini

Mario Fachini is the Founder and CEO at Entrepreneurial Freedom Academy and is a 2-Time #1 Best Selling Author. Mario's first best seller was *Video Marketing for Business Owners: The Ultimate 7 Step Guide to Become The Expert, Authority and Star in Your Niche.* Mario's second #1 best selling book was *The IWDNow Freedom Platform: The World's #1 System to Build Great Looking Wordpress Websites Automatically.* Not only has Mario personally written two #1 Best Selling Books, but he also has a system that guides his clients through writing and publishing a best selling book within 8 weeks.

Chris: Mario, I want to thank you for taking time out of your busy schedule to visit with us today.

Mario: It is a wonderful day and I'm excited to share with your audience to help them.

Chris: Thanks, Mario. Before we get started, can you give us a brief background of Mario Fachini?

Mario: Ever since I was young, I always had a passion for helping people. I originally thought I'd be a doctor lawyer, FBI, CIA, all kinds of different things and when I was in college, I settled on I wanted to have fun, make money and help people and own a company. I changed my plans around a little bit and went into video production and marketing. That led me to having the opportunity to speak to audiences, write a couple of books. Now, I get to hit my goal everyday and live my goal by helping people.

Chris: That's awesome. Mario, tell us a little bit about your current business model.

Mario: I have 2 sides of my business. One is my teaching and training. I work with entrepreneurs, successful people all around the world and I train them on how to become the CEO of their business in life. That doesn't mean you have to be the CEO of a $500 million Fortune 500 company, the CEO to me is the mindset. There's a lot of people that have a business, but they don't see themselves as the business owner. They have the skill set, they started the business, so technically they have a business but they're still doing day-to-day stuff, running themselves ragged and that to me is not a life. What I enjoy training them is how to think properly, set up leveraging systems in their business through my coaching and training, and just really systematize, and teach them how to be the CEO of their business in life. That's where I got the name for the Entrepreneurial Freedom Academy. The second part is my WordPress website builder software. My background is with web design, originally years ago. It's what I started out with. Again, my love of efficiency and systems, and making stuff better so you can spend time with your family and friends, I created a software to be able to build WordPress websites automatically in under 4 minutes. Instead of spending 20 hours nit-picking, you can have your staff do it a lot quicker and then all of you can get back to your family and friends.

Chris: With those 2 sides of your business, I know that keeps you busy, but I also know that it really keeps you focused on helping people.

Mario: Absolutely. I'm thankful for the experience of going through the day-to-day realizing I don't like it and I was either smart enough, if you ask some people or stubborn enough if you ask other people. I was like I don't want to be 30, 35, 40, 50, 60, 70 and not be happy. I started my business when I was 18, so I just knew in the future at some point when I'm older and I have a wife and kids, I'd rather spend time with them, and my family, and friends, and loved ones than sit there nit-picking, freaking out over color palettes and stuff. It doesn't matter, help people serve them, use the gifts God gave you and don't worry about the details is my philosophy.

Chris: I love it. Mario, you are a 2-time bestselling author. When you started thinking about writing your first book, was it a bolt of lightning that hit you or did it just come to you gradually?

Mario: The opposite. I'll go with that. It wasn't a bolt of lightning and then came gradually. It was, I had a few ideas I was marinating around and then the bolt of lightning came. I was playing around with subject matter. I felt I could honestly teach them that I felt competent enough and there's a couple of areas. Then I was giving a speech locally in person, in real life and I was brought into speak on video marketing. I was just having so much fun with that, I was like this is what I should be writing my first book on and that's how it came to be.

Chris: Was that the tipping point for you to say, "Okay, I'm going to write and publish this book"?

Mario: It was definitely that because I have an extensive background in video production. I started off just with the love of video and wanting to be an actor and just make movies. I studied video production in college. I know special effects, editing, shooting, lighting, photography, all the stuff that goes behind the scenes. Then as I progressed through it, I even was selling commercials for Comcast TV ads. All the aspects you generally think of with video, I realized you could be using it for marketing. My strategy in video marketing is a holistic approach because it's not just shoot a video for the sake of shooting a video and then only use it for marketing. There's simple tricks I can show people with lighting. Let me rephrase that, simple knowledge. It's not even a trick. It's just knowing what the heck you're doing. Some of it is a high end way. Some of it is a cheap way that I've used something as simple as my first client, in his restaurant. I used the napkin in place of a soft box to filter the light to get a better picture and use them as website for 2 years.

Chris: Wow. Little tricks. Let me ask this question, Mario. What was the process you went through to write and eventually publish that first book?

Mario: Truthfully, a lot of crying and motivation and believing because it was quite a struggle, I always had a natural talent for helping others and getting them to believe in themselves, but I think we all suffer from being our own worst critic. Maybe not you, but my case, I had a self-esteem issue. I failed English 6 times. Playing that story in my head to you're going to be a number one bestselling author, I'm like this is basically like me trying to jump over the Grand Canyon or climb Everest without an oxygen tank or whatever. For me, it was more of an emotional thing. I knew the subject matter like how you're asking me questions, now you could ask me for 10 hours straight anything you want and I'm very confident whether I'm on stage, on the phone, wherever. I'll be able to answer it, but trying to get all that to slow down, to write it into a book with a format and I'm the one doing it, it was a challenge and all then fears, doubts and all that crap crept in there so it was more of I got to keep re-motivating myself just to keep going. Once I got passed that, it was a lot of fun because I knew I could help people on a bigger scale and I knew what it was going to do for me and more importantly for them.

Chris: I'm assuming you self published the book, correct?

Mario: I did.

Chris: What process did you use to publish the book? Was that through Amazon and CreateSpace?

Mario: It was. I used Amazon. I got a training program on how to do it. It was still self-paced, but it is through Amazon, CreateSpace, and it's what I teach my clients now and I've worked with other people now that I know how to do it. I've helped them publish their book and it's probably my favorite thing to do at this point because it's great in so many levels. I have told people it's like being naked in front of everyone because you have your whole story. Anything you put out there for anyone to read, 24/7, anywhere, they can just get that information on me. It's also freeing at the same time because you no longer have anything to hide because what I realized from taking some other classes on emotional intelligence and leadership, you have nothing to hide any point in time.

Chris: On that first book, what were the biggest surprises you had good or bad when you went through that process?

Mario: Biggest surprise, bad. I didn't realize how emotionally taxing it would be. Biggest surprise, good. The end result was better than what I even thought it could be. It still is. This is on a book I did. We're coming up on 4 years and it's still paying dividends.

Chris: That's awesome. When you published the book, how long did it take you to reach number 1 on Amazon?

Mario: Through the process, it takes roughly a day.

Chris: Really? That has got to come as a surprise to the people who are either reading this in the book, who are listening to this on the audio, a day to be a #1 bestseller?

Mario: Absolutely. The reason for that is you want to condense it down to 24-hour period of time. Just like Google has their search algorithm, Amazon also has their own algorithm. The way it works is you have a 24-hour clock to drive as many sales as possible. Consult someone that knows what they're doing is my advice. It's why I enjoy helping people through the process.

I wouldn't recommend anyone trying to do it on their own because there's a lot of nuances, but the short of it is, all you have to do is condense the sales to one day. What I recommend is going 2, 3 weeks out promoting it like crazy beforehand so that when that day comes, everyone is chomping at the bit to buy it, not seeing it for the first time. I didn't even know.

Chris: What impact has that first book had on your business?

Mario: It impacted it because it gave me a wider reach. It gave me a bigger audience and it showed me that I'm capable of more. The first book took me 2 1/2 months to write. My second book took me a day.

Chris: A day? You have got to explain that to our listeners. How did you write a book in a day?

Mario: Honestly, I implemented some of the strategies that I've teach my private clients about hyper focus. I use the concept I came up with a couple of years ago called Block 15 time. A lot of people say, I don't have the time to do anything and I think that's the adult version, respectfully, of my dog ate my homework. We all have 24 hours a day. Most people just don't use it efficient enough. If you think about it differently, there's 96 opportunities a day. If you chunk them into 15 minutes, Block 15 time, put your phone into airplane mode, turn it off, set a timer, a countdown timer so you have a sense of urgency. Maybe put on some music and just go, "I'm going to focus." Even if your house and car are on fire, there's nothing that's going to be that much different 15 minutes from now. You can still focus and do things so much more efficiently. Two things happen. One, you either hit your goal four times faster because if you're going to allow yourself an hour like most people do, you can probably pull it off in 15 minutes or you get in such a zone, you'll keep going. Either way, it's advantageous and anyone can do it.

Chris: How long was it between when you wrote and published your first book and your second book?

Mario: Roughly 2 years. December 28, 2012 and February 5th, 2015. Just over 2 years.

Chris: Obviously one of the big differences between the process of book #1 and book #2 was the length of time it took you to write it. Where there any other differences in the processes between writing and publishing those bestselling books?

Mario: The big difference was I got comfortable and I helped more people in the process. I helped my private clients do the same thing I did. I got really, really, really, really confident in the process. The process wasn't any different. I didn't just understand it, I was very competent with it, like learning to ride a bike. The first time, it's a little bit harder, then you know how to ride it. You're not confident, you just, you're not falling down. Then you start doing tricks and riding backwards and all kind of stuff. My confidence now is I'll just say it's very high.

Chris: What impact was the second #1 bestseller on your business?

Mario: #1 bestseller for the second book was again, more credibility to an even wider audience and it gave me a different subject matter, the first one was video marketing for business owners. The second one is on the freedom platform website building. Now, I'm also excited to be having my third book, and that is for my entrepreneurial freedom academy. The more topics you're known as the expert on, you have variety. You might be known for one thing, but what about this event over here or this interview over here. If they need subject matter on something else, maybe you are competent, but do they see you that way? It's the same exact thing. After I launched the 2nd book, someone goes we love to have you do an interview because obviously you're the expert on websites. In my mind, my first thought was I haven't done websites in years. For me, me personally, I have a staff that does it, my company does it, but I didn't really see myself that way anymore because it's not what I do. I do teaching and training. I'm still competent and know what I'm talking about and they saw that because of it.

Chris: That credibility is so huge. How are you using your bestselling books in your marketing and prospecting efforts?

Mario: One of my favorite things to do is give them out to people. I'm very focused on how can I help you and I love making people smile and gift giving in general. People see it as a gift and you can write a little bit a message in the cover which I always do. From a personal standpoint, it fuels my soul because it's like I get to improve their life and I know it will. If you want to go straight up marketing, it's like a business card with a lot more room to write stuff and they got you for an hour or two.

The best story I have to date was coming back from speaking at a conference in San Diego. I was a little frazzled. I'm looking for a cell phone charger. My phone is about to die, had some complications with the plane and it was a stupid flight. That was late at night and it was dark. I'm just trying to get home and get a snack, calm down and regroup. I wasn't mean or unpleasant, I just was frazzled. I had books in my carry on, I was looking for my charger and I'm looking for the thing to charge my phone on the plane. That was my focus. I sit down, start talking to a nice lady. She asked what I do. We talked for 3 or 4 minutes before the plane took off. We didn't really talk that much but in those 3, 4 minutes, "My name is Mario. I just spoke in San Diego," this and that. She goes, "Really? I've been wanting to get into that. She goes, "What do you speak on?" I said, "Marketing and I published a book on video marketing," this and that. She's like, "Really? I've always wanted to publish a book." I give her a copy of mine just to show her and she goes, "Can I read it?" "Yeah, sure." I'm still concerned about plugging in my phone. An hour later, she leans over and starts laughing, nudges me on the arm. She's like, "This has been a great flight. It's been such a pleasure getting to know you." Turns back, starts reading the book again. I'm thinking we talked for 4 minutes, the same way you would on a grocery line. No one has ever said that to me. She had been getting to know me through the book for the last hour and the same personality I'm using with you here, I write the book the same way. I wasn't trying to sound fancy or anything. I'm me. I don't try to be anyone else and I wrote it that way. When we got off, she goes, "Here's 20 bucks. I want to keep it. Give me a call. I want to get a book published and I want to learn more." We went our separate ways. I was still concerned about my plug and other stuff. I mean, you could look at that as selling, as marketing, as very low effort. I mean, the benefits were just all encompassed just because I had a copy to give out to her. I didn't expect any of that. It wasn't my goal. She just asked about it. I thought that she'd look at it. She volunteered she wanted to read it.

Chris: What a great story. I know you do a lot of speaking. Do you tend to give copies of your books in your speaking engagements?

Mario: Speaking engagements, I sell them. It depends. I give out a lot and I sell a lot. At the speak engagements, I mean, you can buy them. When I meet someone or if they're interested, it depends on the scenario. I just don't randomly give them out to everyone just for no reason. You want to make sure they'll appreciate it and they'll actually read it. I sell them and give them out. It just depends.

Chris: Mario, you mentioned that lady who said she wanted to write a book. How are you helping others write and publish your books in your current practice?

Mario: That is what I do with my entrepreneurial freedom academy with my private and group coaching clients. I take them through the process that I went through because I had one demographic and then once I started speaking and published my books, my business really changed. My business is completely different so it's so phenomenal and I've really compressed the whole thing down and now in 8 weeks we go through. If you're an expert and authority, you want a bigger audience, you want better positioning, there's so many benefits and it's quite voluminous. I'm not going to try and name them all here, but anyone that wants to grow their business exponentially and make it easier and more profitable, you can do all that by publishing a book, doing videos and doing different things with publicity, all highly leveraged that you do it one time and keep playing dividends for years. Here's the thing, if you don't want to go back and change the book, fantastic. If you do, you can. I don't need to rewrite the book but I've gone back and updated it with new and current information to stay current for the best benefit of everyone. If I didn't, no one is forcing me to. I'm still going to get calls either way.

Chris: Now, you had mentioned 8 weeks. Is that the length of time that you walked somebody through from "hello, I want to write a book" to getting it published?

Mario: I got to be honest. This was part of my own little personal goal because even when I didn't know what I was doing, it took me 2 1/2 months. That was kind of a giant learning curve. There isn't a single client of mine that I've had that it's taken longer than 3 months. Some of it has been with holidays and stuff with their families coming up. Life is not perfect. As I'm always looking for efficiencies and systems and this and that, I was like there's no one including myself when I didn't know what I was doing that's taken longer than 3 months with weekly accountability in different things and motivation. It'll take longer if you're trying on your own, but I've never taken more than 3 months. I started running some numbers and boiling stuff down and go I really don't even think we need 3 months to do this. I think I can do it in 8 weeks. I redid the curriculum and that's what it is right now. If anyone want to get their book published and want more publicity and positioning, I can do it in 2 months.

Chris: When you first tell somebody that, do they just say something like there's no way it could be done in 2 months?

Mario: Quite a bit. That just shows me that it's not the process and it's not me. Like I said earlier, don't take it personal. I have fun with it instead of crying now. It just goes to where their belief is. I mean, when you first learn to ride a bike or drive a car, do anything, it's this giant mountain. Then it's so funny because our human tendency is you might sit there and be fearful or have doubt or whatever the case maybe and the second you do it, guess what you're an expert of and you're telling everyone how great you are at it. You're laughing right?

Chris: It's so true. Mario, here's a question I have for you, can you give us an example of maybe how one of your clients are using their book to help grow their business?

Mario: Absolutely. I'll give you an example of my client, Lori. She is one the greatest people I know and I don't say that lightly because I know a lot of great people. I'd like to think I'm positive but every single time we would talk, every week, she's telling me personal stuff and then this is going on and duh, duh, duh, duh, duh, but I'm still moving forward. She told me some things that I don't know if I'd be able to get through as flawlessly and gracefully she did. Lori, when she was 12, lost her hand in a meat grinder. No one knew this. I meet her. She was referred to someone else and I get a lot of referrals and appreciate them from everyone and I'm thankful but I get a referral. I help her out. My friend knows she's in good hands and she is. I start helping her and we didn't know each other. She never saw me speak. She didn't read my book. She just trusted the referral. I am helping her. I'm learning to get to know her and she's telling me all this. She's interracial, grew up in a mixed family, in the '60s during a time of that's not really the norm, loses her hand when she's 12 in a meat grinder. Has all these life difficulties, divorce, this, that, the other thing. I'm not going to go into

114

all of it. The book is great. It's called Taking My Hand Out of My Pocket.

Now, I'm charged with helping this wonderful woman, pull all this together. Halfway through the training, she goes, "I have got to thank you. I feel so free." I go, "What for?" She goes, "I've lived here in Grand Rapids, Michigan for 18 years I believe." She goes, "No one knows I have a prosthetic." I go, "What?" She goes, "I don't tell most people. The only reason I'm telling you is because you're helping me and it's part of the story and we need it in the book." I go, "You're telling me, I know this and there's people you were with earlier today in person and you'll be with tomorrow and they don't know?" She goes, "Yes." This wasn't just I have something to offer and share my story of inspiration and hope, this was like a transformation in this weight off her shoulder. She would go on finish the book, have a very creative cover. She goes on and immediately, starts telling people and she was able to book speaking gigs, people want her to come to their events. One was called The Failure Lab. They sought her out to speak among some other celebrities that were going to be there. I was just so proud of her. One of my other clients has a radio show and I was able to get her on that. It opens up so many doors on so many levels, it's just so wonderful. No one is deserving of it more. Everyone has something to offer but I'm looking for really great people that have great stories that are making a difference and that is what she is doing.

Chris: She obviously has a great story and as a result of the book, it's now catapulted her into a whole different stratosphere when it comes to what the message that she wants to give to people and at the same time, she's probably making money doing it.

Mario: What's so great is especially with the book, you don't need to knock on doors, you don't need to make cold calls and everything and there's nothing wrong with that. I am not putting them down, I've done everything. Not just my company. I mean, literally, I've done it. I've done calling. I've done doors. I've done everything up until this point and there's nothing better because even if you can breakthrough, you don't have the authority in positioning. You could say it's a numbers game and you might win because you're more aggressive but there's no way. You might have your foot in the door but you don't have the positioning to get through to the top. The only time you get that positioning is after you've completely successfully helped them through the process. Short of having the authority positing of a book and speaking to audiences, prospecting can be tough.

Chris: I can't think of a better mechanism than a book to establish that credibility and that authority. And to your earlier point, is that lady, after an hour of reading your book felt that she knew you and that's just so awesome.

Mario: What else is great is I'm feeling that someone listening to this is going, "Wow, that sounds great, but I don't know about me. That sounds difficult. I don't like writing." I failed English 6 times, but here's the thing. Nowadays, you don't need to lock yourself in a cabin. There's this thing called the smart phone. The same way I'm talking right now, you can talk into it and guess what you do? You get it transcribed and turn that into a book. Even better, shoot a video like my book suggests, Video Marketing for Business Owners. Shoot a video, get the audio taken out, transcribed. Turn that into a book and now you have a cool video also to do other stuff with. You can leverage it. There is nothing that is more efficient that gives you the bang for your buck for the time invested that is so multifaceted. Even beyond that, even if you had to write it with pen and paper, it would still be worth it but you don't. You could talk for 2 or 3 hours and have a book.

Chris: Mario, I think that is such great advice because so many people I talk to about the concept of writing a book, it's "oh, I could never write a book." You've just given 2 ideas where they don't have to "write a book" but they can talk the book or they can film the book if you will, have it transcribe and they now have a book.

Mario: Chris, can I share something else with you to that end?

Chris: Absolutely.

Mario: I needed to get myself motivated and like I was saying with Block 15 time, just reframe and rethink about stuff. My first chapter, not the whole chapter but I was driving to another speaking engagement and I picked up my phone went into Evernote. Have you heard of Evernote?

Chris: Yes, I have.

Mario: Did you know that your phone, you can do voice-to-text on it?

Chris: I am aware of that.

Mario: If you have Evernote, open voice-to-text is basically an automatic transcription service and it's free.

Chris: You got to love it.

Mario: I just prompt up the phone, sit it on the arm rest or whatever and I literally said something. I should see if I can find this note because I told this story and people laughed. I'm like, "No, I'm being 100% serious." I needed to get the ball rolling. I never thought I'm going to write 12 chapters right now, but I have 15 minutes before I get to my destination, what can I do to be productive? I just started talking the same way you would in a Bluetooth, maybe get fancy, hook it to your phone, whatever, this is me. This is this moment. I just started talking the way I am now and I was like, "This is interesting. I don't like writing. I never liked English and I'm supposed to be writing a book. Oh, look a truck. I'm going to have a good afternoon and so let's get started on the book." I literally, when I went home later, in my notes that said, "Oh, look a truck." It's transcribed everything I was saying. I chuckled. All you have to do is delete that later on. Obviously, you don't put in the final script. Say whatever you want. You could say, "My goal right now is to outline 12 chapters, 10 chapters. Think of a puzzle border. Make the border then fill it in, chunk it up a little bit, add a time. I wasn't trying to finish my book, but you know what, that is when the book got finished because in that moment, me driving while talking to myself like I was going to do anyway, the book got started which means it got finished.

Chris: That's awesome. Mario, what advice would you give to someone who's considering writing a book?

Mario: Do it.

Chris: I love it. Just short and sweet. Mario, what's the best way for somebody to get a hold of you if they wanted to take you up on your challenge of idea to #1 bestselling author in 8 weeks.

Mario: mariofachini.com.

Chris: Perfect. Mario, I really appreciate you taking time out of your schedule today.

Mario: I appreciate you Chris for the opportunity. This was a lot of fun.

You can reach Mario at mario@iwdnow.com. Mario's website is http://mariofachini.com.

CHRIS CARLSON

Jeff Turley

Jeff Turley is the Founder of GoNetYourself. Jeff's company has a unique deliverable and helps individuals and companies grow their business through the use of video.

Chris: Hi, this is Chris Carlson. I'm here today with my good friend Jeff Turley. We're going to talk today about how you can use video in your sales and marketing efforts. Jeff, I want to thank you for taking a few minutes out of your busy schedule to be with me today.

Jeff: Sure, it's great to be here.

Chris: Jeff, we're going to deep dive into how individuals and companies can use video in their sales and marketing efforts, but first, why don't you give us a brief background of Jeff Turley.

Jeff: A brief background is that I had an idea of GoNetYourself while still in the finance world. Never done a video in my life. Didn't even have a passion for that, although I enjoy the storytelling and the marketing part of it. It was really coming out of the idea that people need a lot of video, and they need it quickly, and they need it done very, very well. That's where the idea of GoNetYourself came from. My background really was more in the world of finance, but then I just took a step out into the whole entrepreneurial world. This is what's come of it.

Chris: Tell us a little bit more about GoNetYourself.

Jeff: GoNetYourself, really, at its core is a gym membership for video production. What we've done is

121

made an affordable, repeatable, and executable way for your teams or companies to create a lot of video because in today's world, video has a very short shelf life. You need to do something that's repeatable in many different aspects of your company. It may be sales and marketing. It may be something for your website. It may be stories for your CEO, whatever it is. You need a lot of different video, and you need to be able to do it very quickly and very efficiently.

Chris: When you went back to that moment that was the GoNetYourself idea, was that a bolt of lightning that struck you, or was it something that came to you over time?

Jeff: To tell you the truth, it was really a one-hour conversation with a friend. It just came. We were talking about kind of next things in life. John and I were talking about doing a podcast, actually. Then he talked about how expensive it was to do videos. I said it's got to be done in video. He's like, wow, no, that's way too expensive. I said, oh, that's why people keep sending me really, really bad videos. He said, yeah. All of a sudden, I mean literally, I know exactly where I was standing. I went back to my office that day and wrote out the entire business plan and executed it. Nothing has really changed. It's really been a scalable studio, so that you can create ... again, I'll say it. affordable, repeatable, and executable videos across all segments of your company.

Chris: How long from the time that you wrote the business plan to the doors opening and you have that first video going?

Jeff: About six months.

Chris: Wow.

Jeff: I had to talk my wife into it. She was the one that kind of had to say yes or no to the whole thing, but I showed her the numbers, and I told her what we were doing, and it made sense. We set up the first studio here in Bellevue and got moving in 2012. It's been going well ever since.

Chris: What's been the biggest surprises, either good or bad, during those four years as you've grown this business?

Jeff: Well, because I didn't come out of this, I really came out of the finance world into this world, but I think the biggest surprise is that nobody knows how to do video yet. When the first chief marketing officer came in, I thought that individual would know everything about how to do a video. They were completely clueless. A lot of people feel like, oh, they're way behind the curve. That's just not true. What I've realized is people may have done a video, but usually it's done with a big PR firm where they do everything for them and they write a big check to them. When it comes to, hey, marketing officers or teams within large corporations, they don't really know how to execute a video. That was a surprise to me. I just thought that marketing officers would know what to do. No.

Chris: Would you say that even today people are still struggling with how to do videos?

Jeff: Yes, absolutely. They are struggling not only how to do the video, but how to use the video is probably the biggest struggle. Anybody can do a video. We always say anybody can do a video. You just can't do very many of them if you're going to do them yourself and you don't have a scalable editing platform to do them. But where they're really struggling is, okay, I made my video, and they post and they pray. Then they get like 300 views, and they're, okay, that wasn't worth it. Our focus at GoNetYourself is really not allowing our members to just create a video, but say, hey, how are you going to use these? We have those conversations on the front end a lot more than we've ever had.

Chris: Great, so you talked about your members. Do you have a typical member or are you doing business with all types of companies, all shapes and sizes?

Jeff: They're definitely all shapes and sizes for us because we're very focused on people who can walk in. It's usually the larger corporations, like a Microsoft or a Concur or a T-Mobile where they can just walk into the studio and walk back out. One of our best stories is when Concur used to be in Redmond, and then two years into GoNetYourself they moved in right next door. It's been a great friendship ever since because their executives walk in, walk out. Their videos are done a lot of times in 15 or 20 minutes.

We have this one executive from a large cell phone carrier that does a lot of business with us and that executive lives in the Bravern right next to us, and one day I pull up to the stop sign and there's that executive walking across the street with his coffee in his hand, getting ready to walk into our studio. I meet him in the elevator. We ride up. He walks in, he hits his message, he literally was there for like 20 minutes. He walks out, he thinks it's an awesome thing. That's really our sweet spot, when you're close to one of our studios, and you can use it as your studio. The name isn't a joke. The name is exactly what we do. We're giving you all the tools, all the lights, all the cameras, all the prompters, all the production that you need, all the editing to create a scalable video strategy for your team.

Chris: That person just has to come in and perform, if you will, and you guys take care of the rest.

Jeff: Pretty much, pretty much. We help them with the scripts. We help them polish their scripts. We give them the tools on how to do those scripts. Usually, scripts are we always say they're 150 words. If you don't know 150 words of your message, you better go get a PR firm. Most people know that it's the 150-300 words that they need to write. Then we help them polish that down to what we call their video voice. A lot of times people know how to say it, but once they get in front of the camera, they're like, oh no. They don't how to say it in such a quick sound bite. It's very hard to do.

Chris: What are some of the ways that your members are using the videos, be it training, or sales, or marketing, or whatever?

Jeff: That goes back to the tool. How do you use it? Early on, in late 2012, T-Mobile came in and sat across the table from me. The person said, "I want five." I thought, "Okay, you want five dollars worth of video? Fifty dollars? What do you want?" He goes, "No, I want five memberships because I want one to lower call volume at T-Mobile to our call centers. It was right then. He goes, "I want one for each one of our devices. I want them in different languages." I was like, "Oh wow, okay. I get it. He gets it." It's all over the board. Instead of using video just as a marketing piece like it was before, it was just, hey, I got a video and I use it on my website, and there it is. It's there for three years because we just paid ten grand for it.

Instead, I'm saying, okay, you need video testimonials, you need CEO messaging, you need executive messaging. Internal communications is huge, huge, huge, for any large organization. If your organization is more than 200, 300 people, then you need internal communications, you need live webinars. We do live webinars. They use it for all different types of things. Now, how they use it, that can be posting on LinkedIn, posting on Facebook, buying ads on Google. We just got off the phone with a large company, and they're using the videos to post it and buying ads on Facebook. They can do that.

That's kind of a media marketing blitz you can use them for, but I always say the best way to use video is, tell your story authentically and tell it again and again and again and repeat that story. Then, if you can, we talk a lot about amplification of your video. Use and leverage your teams to use that social message. If you have a CEO that's telling you a message, get everybody to post it on all of their social networks. For a large company, that's going to be harder to do. If you're a small company, then you just have the CEO message, but then you can leverage all their LinkedIns, all their Facebooks, all of their Instagrams with that video. That's how you use it as a tool.

The second aspect would be story. How are you telling really, really good stories? Once you get a good story, you can use it over and over. You can use that story in a blog. You can use it on your website. You can then reuse it for a different blog a year later. I've done one story, and I've probably used it ten different times. Lots of different ways.

Chris: Authenticity, great use of stories, and I'll put some words in your mouth, re-purpose, repurposing your videos.

Jeff: Repurposing your videos all the time. We've got one CEO that she just did a video that was the intro to one of her speeches that she was doing in Germany. We did this great video, and then it was done so well that they ended up using it as the front page of their website. They repurposed it. They spend ten grand on doing what we call primos, which is a higher animation video, as her intro right before she walked onto the stage. It was done so well, then they used it for their website. She got two uses out of it.

Chris: Jeff, before we get out of here today, why don't you give me a great example of how one of your members is using video.

Jeff: We call them our super members. Our super members have figured out a philosophy at GoNetYourself that we call the flirt, the fix, and the forward. The flirt is that hook where you're only giving them 30 seconds or a minute and a half. It may be funny. It may be cute. It may be whatever, but you hooked me because I like you and that's what we call the flirt.

Then the fix is you're moving them down to the next step and that is you've given them something free, some "how to" free information. That free information is how most millennials and most people search on the internet. How to do something, right. That's the fix, right.

Then, after that, you move them into the forward, forwarding deeper into whatever you want to sell them or communicate with them. There's a deeper, longer video. There's kind of three ways to move them along the sales cycle through video. The flirt, the fix, and the forward. We've seen several teams out of Concur and T-Mobile use that very, very effectively.

Chris: I can't think of a better way that a salesperson or a marketing organization could use video than using the three F's, the Flirt, the Fix and the Forward.

Jeff: Yeah, absolutely.

Chris: Well, Jeff, thanks for your time. I really do appreciate it.

Jeff: Thank you.

Jeff can be reached at jturley@gonetyourself.com. Their website is http://gonetyourself.com

David Brooke

David Brooke is The Gratitude Guy. David has built a business from nothing and he did it speaking everywhere and anywhere.

Chris: David, I want to thank you for taking time out of your busy schedule to meet with me today.

David: You bet, happy to, Chris.

Chris: Well, David, I know we're going to talk a lot about how are you using speaking in your prospecting efforts, but before we do that deep dive, why don't you give us a brief background of David Brooke?

David: Yes, thank you Chris. My background was, when I was 19 years old, I'd done a little talk for a teacher of mine, and when I went to the car later that day, I remember thinking I want to be a speaker some day. Well, took me over 40 years to get to that particular place in life, I had done retail and a lot of other things, but I always knew I wanted to be a motivational speaker. I wasn't quite sure what the speaking topic would be, but it would be around motivation.

It wasn't until my early 60s I finally said, "You know what, it's time to stand up and do this," and I started this 3 or 4 years ago, and when we talk about speaking gigs or speaking engagements as we will in a minute, it's just something that had been with me forever. I'm glad I finally got into this because I've got to impact lives, which is kind of in my two word motto if you will, and that's how I got into it. It was always about helping people.

Chris: Well, it's really interesting. A question I always like to ask people is when they finally decided to do that next step, in this case, the Gratitude Guy, I always ask them, was it something that was a bolt of lightning or something that took time? Nobody has ever told me it took 40 years.

David: Yeah, it's been a long time. The Gratitude Guy came about eventually or evolved through time. Mainly when I talk about the motivation piece is that I had a number of tragedies happen in my life, and I was looking for something to help me. Somebody said, "You need to get a gratitude journal, and you need to start thinking with a gratitude mind-set." That's how it evolved and I started writing in a gratitude journal, eventually I started doing videos about gratitude, and really understood the power of a gratitude mind-set, or an attitude of gratitude if you will.

As that moved forward, one day I came to someone that said, "You're the Gratitude Guy, you are the guy that speaks about gratitude." Oh, the Gratitude Guy, maybe that will be a little handle that I use, and that's how The Brooker - That Gratitude Guy came about.

Chris: That was the impetus to making this a full time business then?

David: Yes, correct. Part of it, it sounds a bit dramatic, but really, I look at it as kind of something that saved my life, because I had enough tragedy that I thought I'm going to need some tools and I speak to groups about getting another tool in the tool kit. For me, I thought I am going to have to have something, because I would get depressed, and I would see everything I *didn't* have in my life versus what I *did* have. And being a motivational speaker is great, but I wanted to have, as I said, a handle or something I was really passionate about, and in my embracing gratitude I went, "Wow, this helps me focus on everything I have, versus what I don't have." I will say it to groups many times, Chris, it really did change and transform, and in many cases saved my life, by adopting that mind-set.

Chris: Not only has it helped people that you've coached and spoke to, but it's helped you immensely.

David: Absolutely. And I think about the line, when the student is ready, the teacher will appear. I think sometimes I walk away from audiences that have gotten bigger and bigger now, feeling as energized, as motivated as I've ever been, and I think, wait, who got more from this, them or me? A lot of times it's just as much for me as it is for the group of people I'm speaking to.

Chris: That's awesome. Well, David, tell us a little bit about your business model, the combination of your coaching and your speaking.

David: I think what had happened initially is remember, I always wanted to be a speaker, and as I said, that went back to when I was 19. I remember talking to people, we all are people who get mentored or mentor people ourselves, and somebody said, "Well, you need to do a talk, you need to get a speech put together." The way that it started with me, I thought, let me get 5 modules together, and it was going to be the 5 things I talk about with gratitude, and I'm going to have to get speaking engagement, so I took what I thought was a pretty reasonable route. I'll go talk to Rotary, I'll go talk to Kiwanis, I'll talk to Lions Clubs, I'll talk to Chambers of Commerce, I'll talk to anybody I can. Churches, old folks homes if you will, nursing homes, but I thought I got to have the 5 modules.

That was very important to me. in my case it was Embrace Gratitude number 1, It Takes As Long As It Takes, Never Give Up was number 2. Number 3 was Clear Out Your Brain And Make Room For Gratitude. Number 4 is a Gratitude Journal and number 5 is Sharing Gratitude. Then, I was kind of coached along the way, "You need to do a book, it would be helpful to do a book." Then your book is kind of your speech and your speech is your book. So, those were the 5 modules and then the book takes those 5 modules and just expands on them into a lot more detail with exercises and little stories to illustrate the point, little points, little quotes and things that might speak to something I'm talking about. But it really has been the speaking that has driven the business more than anything else, because that is getting out there.

There are a number of people I know that have written books, which I've been always very impressed with, but they've got a garage full of books, and that doesn't do them any good. I sell more books in my speaking engagements than anything else and I get coaching clients there, so I'm such a believer in having a book. But I do the speaking engagements because that leads to all sorts of other opportunities.

Chris: To include your coaching, is that correct?

David: Yes, correct. I will mention that too. At the end of my talks, I ask if I can make a quick comment on what do I do. And I'll mention I have my books for sale, I offer individual and group coaching, I also am always looking for workshops and other opportunities, so please come up and speak to me afterwards, so it's great.

These people are already feeling really good about who you are, and now they're even more inclined to want to come up and talk to you, maybe even before they met you.

Chris: You mentioned all those places that you gave talks to. What did you do to proactively solicit those talks, so somebody would say, "Come in and give us a talk?" I know some of them were complimentary, and some of them were paid. What was your marketing plan for those?

David: The vast majority of them were complimentary, and this is something that now, I always joke about living on macaroni and cheese the last few years as I built the business. But I thought well let's see, if you got Rotaries, we got Kiwanis and Lions Club and Chambers as I mentioned earlier. Well, what's the easiest way to find those, the Internet. I would go in, and I would look up Rotaries, I would look up all those various service groups, find out who they were, e-mail them. I did a little flyer, The Brooker - That Gratitude Guy and the speech was called Happiness Starts with Gratitude, my talk is 20 to 30 minutes, a little bit about the speech or the talk, and a couple of sentences on how this can change your mind-set, a couple of little take-a-ways somebody might get having a different mindset, using the gratitude journal, becoming more happy or less depressed or whatever, and then a little bio.

I would take that flyer as I called it, and I would send it out to those people, and they would e-mail me back and say, "We would like you to talk on such and such a date." That's one thing that was huge. The other one was just picking up the phone. "ABC Rotary, this is Chris." "Hi Chris, Dave Brooke, I'm known as The Gratitude Guy and I'd love to come and speak to your group," and so on. Like anything, in the beginning it was challenging because gosh, people don't call you back, they don't e-mail you back, but when you're so passionate, and I bring this up a lot, another module I recently had, it was called Find yourself, Find your Passion, Find your Purpose, if you're really passionate about something, getting hung up on or

133

not returned calls or an e-mail doesn't get returned, doesn't really bother you. You just keep pressing forward, because you're very passionate about what you're talking about.

Chris: You moved from giving all these talks complimentary, to getting paid a lot of money, as you and I have talked about, for giving talks.

David: Correct.

Chris: What are you doing now to get the paid speaking engagements?

David: A very good friend of mine said you need to do speaking, you need to get books, and then you need to get referrals. I don't know who that was, but it was a great line. I think that, as it shifted to the paid relationships or the paid gigs as we call them, I thought I never want to lose sight of the free ones. As an example, to anybody who is listening or reading, I think I'm at 250 or 260 talks in the last 3 years. It's not quite, 3-4 a week, so that's a lot of talks, and 90% of those are free.

However, I cannot tell you how many paid gigs came out of one of those free talks. We'd like you to come and speak to our national convention, we want you to do so and so. I don't think I'll ever get away from them, plus, when you're really passionate about your subject, whether it's gratitude or what have you, the more people I get in front of, the better, because if it helps one person, that's one more than yesterday. I can think of some of these where people come up and they buy the journals, plus you sell your books there, you always sell more in the speaking circuit, because you have this authenticity.

People want to take you home, that's what they say, "I want to take a piece of this person home." They want to get the book, and they want to get the journal, and they want to do that type of thing. I think what's happened is, you also get a reputation, and that's, "You got to hear this Chris guy speak, you got to hear this Dave guy speak," and the only way you can do that is to be speaking. Then they tell other people and then they tell other people. But that's why I don't think I'll ever get away from the free speeches, but it might have gone from 80-20 free to now 20-80 or something like that.

It's nice to realize the income that comes with this, and you become more confident in yourself, and more passionate, and honestly, in a lot of ways, a better speaker too. Everyone of those free speeches makes you a better performer, or a better presenter.

Chris: I think it's fair to say that speaking has just been incredible for your business.

David: Oh, absolutely, couldn't agree more.

Chris: You shared with me something, that in 2015 you doubled your income, is that correct?

David: Yeah, well you know, when you double a nickel it's 10 cents.

Chris: You're being very modest, David.

David: This year, it's going to go from 10 to 20 cents, so that's still good. Yeah, and thank you for asking. I think the thing that's interesting to me is that the money is a by-product. Years ago, I read a book by Marshall Sinclair and it was called *Do What You Love, The Money Will Follow*. I remember reading the book, but the title kind of said it all. I remember thinking, if I have a great connection with myself and I want to change lives, which is what I want to do, and then I find something I'm passionate about, which was speaking, motivational speaker, pushing gratitude if you will, embracing a gratitude mind-set to help you through all aspects of your life, then you will find your purpose.

I noticed when you find your purpose, generally you get paid pretty well for that, but in my opinion, it has to be in that sequence.

Chris: I want to recap what we talked about, you put together, very strategically and through passion, a series of talks, and then you did something that the vast majority of people don't do. You went out there and you worked to get these engagements.

David: Correct.

Chris: It wasn't just throw it up on a website, or put it on Facebook, or put it on LinkedIn and think that just because it's there people are going to come.

David: Right.

Chris: You went out and you did the hard work that so many people are unwilling to do.

David: Correct.

Chris: By doing that, you got the speaking engagements, some paid, some not paid, and it has morphed into a great business.

David: Yes, and I would add one more thing, Chris. A part of that which is so important, and I know you and I talked about this, it is so important, you've got to have phenomenal follow-through. I mean, yes, I went out and I would call these people multiple times, send e-mails multiple times, I'd send a follow up e-mail, "Just making sure you got my e-mail," "Just wanted to make double sure you got my e-mail." "Sorry Mr. Brooke, it went to Spam, we didn't get it, yes we'd like to have you come and speak." There's the great line as the sales coach, you know this too, the average number of sales calls it takes to make a sale is 4, the average number of sales calls it takes a salesman to get discouraged is 2, so there's always the will you hang tough for the 4 calls and not get discouraged at the 2.

That's why I like the passion piece, because to me, it was difficult and there were days when it was really discouraging, but if you just keep at it and you follow through, good things will happen. And I'll mention one other thing. Just came up the last week since you and I have talked. I met 3 or 3 people recently that I needed to connect with. It could be a coaching thing, it could be a speaker, it could be a speaking gig, it could be any number of things. Before I even wait for them, I e-mailed them, and each one of these people, the first thing they put in their e-mails, "Thank you so much for reaching out so quickly." That's follow through.

That's back to the passion, you're passionate about it, and you won't wait for somebody else to call you. Or as you said, the coffee meeting, the lunch meeting, everybody in my opinion doing what we're doing should have at least 1, or 2, or 3, or 4 coffee/lunches every week with somebody new, because there's always somebody you never know how that might blossom. It might be just a new friend, but sometimes I am having coffee with somebody and they ask, "Would you ever consider speaking for so and so?"

"No." "Can I have this guy call you?" That's just how it works sometimes.

Chris: Great things happen then, right?

David: Yeah.

Chris: Well, David, I know there's going to be people who are reading this or listening to this that are going to want to reach out to you for one or two reasons. Number 1, to find out a little bit more about The Gratitude Guy, and Number 2 what they might want to do is hire you to come in and speak, so what's the best way for them to get in contact with you?

David: Thank you, Chris. The easiest way is my website. TheBrooker.com, that's where I have my videos and a lot of coaching opportunities and things there, as well as my e-mail is thebrooker@thebrooker.com. That's the easiest one of all, so for anything, and just as I finished saying, I always get back to people the same day when they e-mail me.

Chris: Well, hopefully what they do is they go to your website and they subscribe to your YouTube channel, so they can get that weekly gratitude video.

David: I have the YouTube channel there, I have my 2 minute weekly video, I have a lot of other videos there, the coaching, the books are available there, so pretty much everything you want is there. I might add too, on that website, when they look at it, I chose to do a walk on video where I actually walk on the screen, "Hi, I'm the Brooker, That Gratitude Guy." Not everybody will agree with that, but I really like it, because when you're a speaker, whether it's Chris or Dave or whoever, when you can see the person and the video walks come on in the first couple of seconds, you immediately get a flavor of their style, of their energy, of their look, of their gestures and so forth, so that's what you'll notice in that video when on the website, it's very effective.

Chris: I encourage everybody to go to that website. David, thanks for your time today.

David: You're welcome, thank you Chris.

David can be reached at thebrooker@thebrooker.com. His website is http://www.thebrooker.com

Brian Haner

Brian Haner is CEO of Image Source, a full service, branded merchandise and apparel agency located in Kirkland, WA. He is the best Business Development person I have ever met. Brian is truly amazing when it comes to asking for and receiving referrals.

Chris: Hi. I'm Chris Carlson. I'm here today with my good friend, Brian Haner, CEO of Image Source. We're going to talk about how Brian uses referrals to generate revenue. So, Brian, first of all, thanks for taking time out of your schedule to visit with me.

Brian: You're welcome, Chris.

Chris: Brian, give us a brief background of Brian Haner.

Brian: My background in the promotional marketing industry stems, from 24 years ago. I started 24 years ago working for another agency. About 6 years into that I decided, hey, I think I can do this bigger and better and I started Image Source out of my upstairs bedroom of my house, believe it or not. That was 18 years ago and today we're headquartered in Kirkland, Washington, 37 employees, and revenue in excess of $15 million annually. We've had quite a ride.

Chris: Awesome. Well, let's go back in time a little bit. What were the early days like, in terms of prospecting?

Brian: Back in the early days, realize that there was no social media, there was no LinkedIn. There were not a lot of these online tools and resources that we have today. Back then, it was kind of the good old fashioned way

141

where I was telling my story to everybody. I had my business cards in my pocket and everybody that I would see, I would tell my story to. That's how I prospected. Even at times when, after hours, when I'm with my wife or my family, I'm still prospecting at night, at dinner, and I'm running into people and you want to make sure that you're continuously telling your story. I think that's the way that helped me and my success early on.

Chris: I've known you for several years and you're masterful at networking and getting referrals. Was it always like that, or was that something you had to learn as you grew as a sales person?

Brian: Getting referrals is a little bit different than building relationships. I was always good at building relationships and creating the loyalty with suppliers and clients and business people and building trust as well. I think that always came pretty easy, but asking for referrals isn't always the same thing, because you're asking somebody to help you out, right? You're asking somebody to refer you to some other person. I think what I've realized is that it took me a little time. There's some skill involved in it, but it took me a little time to realize the power of it and how intentional you have to be to do that. It's okay to ask for referrals and it's okay to tell people, "I need your help, I want you to refer me to somebody because I'm trying to grow my business." I think that's okay.

Chris: Isn't it amazing how many sales people are so reluctant to ask for that help?

Brian: Absolutely.

Chris: Well, on a daily or weekly basis, what goes through your mind in terms of, "I've got to get some referrals today or this week?"

Brian: If you're driving revenue for your business, which is my primary goal, and realizing how powerful referrals are, you have to do it consistently, right? For me, I do it on a weekly basis. I probably spend 2-3 hours a week on asking for referrals. Most of that comes through LinkedIn, but there's also a part of that that is me calling on current clients and people I know, asking them for referrals. You have to be purposeful with that, you have to know how powerful that is and use it to your advantage.

Chris: I know you have many sales people in your organization. What's the difference that you see in those that are successful generating referrals and those that are not so successful in generating referrals?

Brian: I think, first, is having the courage to ask for the referral, just like I mentioned a couple of minutes ago. I think especially the newer people, sometimes they don't have that courage to ask for it, or they're worried about, "Hey, this isn't the right time to ask for it. I'm not quite ready for that. They don't trust me as much." I think the key is just creating an urgency in that. Referrals are so powerful and I think people should use them as their, especially as a sales person, as their primary marketing tool out there. It's probably the most cost-effective marketing tool, too, to actually ask for referrals and build your referral network up.

Chris: How important is it that sales people have goals for referrals, either a weekly, or monthly basis?

Brian: For us it's really important, I mean, all of our sales team are required to ask for a certain amount of referrals each week. Then we track those referrals and how they actually align with future proposals and future orders and things like that. I think it's really important. I think what happens is once people realize the power of referrals, when they start seeing a great return and business opportunities and relationship building and all these things that come your way after asking for a referral, when they see the value of it, they respect it much more.

Chris: For the younger sales people, do you find, sometimes, that maybe they ask too early?

Brian: Sometimes they ask too early, sometimes they ask too late, right? I think I see it both ways. When they ask too early, they may not be thinking about the state of the relationship that they're in. They may be asking too early, where the person they're asking might not be comfortable or they might be reluctant to give them a referral based on the fact that they've known them for a short period of time or there's not a relationship established. On the flip side of that, sometimes people want to wait too long because they think the client is not quite ready for me to ask for a referral yet. There is a right time and everybody has a different right time to ask. Sometimes people wait too long to ask, where they could actually do it sooner than later.

Chris: Is it fair to say that most sales people wait too long as opposed to ask too early?

Brian: Yes, sir.

Chris: Before we get out of here, today, Brian, what's the one piece of advice that you would give a sales person when it comes to referrals?

Brian: My piece of advice is when you're sitting in front of somebody, it's not so much asking for the referral, asking for the referral is one thing, but when you actually sit down with a person, after a referral has been made and you're having coffee or having a meeting or whatever you're doing, the key is to make sure that you're adding value to them as well. Often times when people ask for referrals and it's tough for people, because you're asking a favor from somebody, right? You're asking somebody to help you out. At the same time, make sure that you're always adding value to them and you're willing to help them out in any way possible, because when you have that reciprocal relationship, it's a win-win and referrals will come fast and furiously.

Chris: So, add value and the referrals will come.

Brian: Yeah.

Chris: Awesome. Brian, thanks for your time today.

Brian: You got it.

Author's Note: Referrals even played a big part in this interview. Brian and I did our interview in the GoNetYourself studio in Bellevue, WA. I was *referred* to the founder of GoNetYourself, Jeff Turley, by Brian Haner. The studio technician during our interview was *referred* to Jeff Turley by Brian Haner. One of Brian's top salespeople was *referred* to Image Source by Jeff Turley. I have *referred* several clients to Jeff Turley. **REFERRALS WORK!**

You can reach Brian at brian@ImageSourceTeam.com. Their website is www.imagesourceteam.com.

CHRIS CARLSON

Brian Bushlach

Brian Bushlach is Executive Producer and Host of Feedback Media. Brian has used radio in a very unique way to grow his business.

Chris: Hi, I'm Chris Carlson and I'm here with my good friend Brian Bushlach and we're going to talk about how Brian is using radio in his prospecting efforts. So Brian, first of all, thanks for joining me today.

Brian: You bet. Glad to be here, Chris.

Chris: Well Brian, before we dive into what you're doing with radio, why don't you give us a brief background of Brian Bushlach?

Brian: Well, I'm a Northwest native going way back. Born and raised in Madras, Oregon. An Oregon State graduate. Left the area briefly in the early 1990's. Short stint at CBS Sports in New York producing The NFL Today and NBA on CBS. Came back to the west coast to Portland as a sportscaster at Channel 6, the CBS affiliate, for about 10 years and ever since then been in broadcasting, radio; you name it, we've done it.

Chris: So, obviously, you've been doing this awhile?

Brian: Yeah. It's been 30 years this year. Hard to believe. I graduated from high school in '86 and so I had to figure something out at that point. The local radio station had an opportunity to call the local high school basketball games and I needed a job and my dad told me I better pay the rent, so that's how it all started.

Chris: That's seems like a great way to get started. What radio shows are you hosting today?

Brian: We produce and host three radio shows, primarily in the Northwest and on the West Coast. Feedback Media produces a show called Sip Northwest Live, which is a syndicated wine show that airs on twelve stations around the Northwest. Business Briefing, in its twelfth year now, airs in the Seattle and Portland markets. That's a show focused on business owners and executives. Last fall we launched a show called Youity Lifestyle. This is the show that supports my day job in financial services with a company called Youity. Youity Lifestyle focuses on boomers and what they love, like travel, dining, food and wine and all that good stuff.

Chris: Now if I'm not mistaken, Business Briefing was the first of those shows that you launched?

Brian: Yeah, it was. We had a show prior to that called The Home and Wealth Show that we launched 2003, 2004 and I like to joke that became an oxymoron in 2007, 2008. So we were really forced to change the ingredients of that show and at that time shifted to Business Briefing.

Chris: So was Business Briefing an evolution as opposed to the first show or did it just kind of come to you "hey, I want to go right into business?"

Brian: Yeah, we kind of had to rework that show. It got to a point where in 2008 & 2009 the real estate market was in pretty bad shape to talk about home equity. Homes as investment at that point, really didn't resonate with very many people, so I thought of the idea of focusing on business owners and executives. At the time I really felt that the private sector had been overlooked in terms of the public sector, so we launched that show in the Portland market 2009 and it's been success ever since.

Chris: It's a great show.

Brian: Thank you.

Chris: I've had the privilege of being on there a couple times.

Brian: You have.

Chris: Let me ask you this question. What opportunities have you created as a result of hosting the show?

Brian: Lots. I think, you know, it's been an evolution since we first started and I was thinking about monetizing those shows. You know, you hear that saying that you're an overnight success after ten years, right? That's pretty much what it took for us. It really was. The early years were very difficult, particularly during the downturn in 2007, 2008 when there weren't a lot of marketing dollars out there, so you had to be pretty creative and cost effective with your productions. We've been able to really leverage the on-air opportunity for our guests and have built some great clientele. We're working with Delta Airlines now. Expedia is a great client of ours. We're talking to Four Seasons Resorts about a partnership with them. Really, it all starts with just that opportunity to connect with them. You know, really show them what we can do from an on-air perspective and then that really opens up the door for a podcast, which I really think is the future of radio.

Chris: It sounds as though having that radio show is allowing you to get into places that possibly you wouldn't have gotten into otherwise.

Brian: I think so. I think that it definitely opens doors that we probably wouldn't be able to get into if we didn't have that opportunity and sometimes it takes a while to open that door, but now when you can get in the door and show people what you can do and how you can leverage it, it's pretty powerful.

Chris: What's the biggest challenge somebody would have to get into radio, i.e. having a radio show of their own?

Brian: I think being consistent. You hear a lot about podcasting. Maybe it's the flavor of the month or flavor of the week for a lot of people out there and they might do it a couple of times and then run out of gas or run out of topics. You really can't do that. I mean, with any type of media you have to be consistent. Whether it's social media or over the air traditional broadcasts or podcasts, you have to have the content. You have to be able to push out the content. You have to be relevant and it has to be fresh every week. I think for a lot of, for lack of a better word, amateurs out there, that's where they really hit the wall as they don't have that content. They get caught up in their day job and they can't do that day after day and week after week.

Chris: Well assuming they have the content, is there enough air time out there for somebody to go to a station, a local station, and actually go to them and say, "I'd like to have a show on this particular topic?"

Brian: I think there is. The key is really producing a quality show and I think, again, that's where you have to have that expertise. You have to really know how to craft a quality show so that you have engaging content for your listeners. Because in today's environment with commercial radio it's a pay to play model. If you're going to pay to play, you better have great content and you better have a good ROI on what you're putting out there or it just won't pencil.

Chris: When you mention podcasting, let's talk about the relationship between the radio show and podcasting. How are you using podcasting in conjunction with your radio shows?

Brian: Well for us it's seamless. A lot of the content that we use over the year can be re-purposed as a podcast. In going into it from a production standpoint, I will tape the shows like they're live, like they're a podcast, and then we can edit that material for our Business Briefing show, for our Youity Show, in some cases for our wine show. Now, there's a lot of times where I'll tape specifically for a specific show. If we're at a winery, it's probably going to be for the wine show. If we're with a business executive the same holds true. It's probably going to be for the business show. If there's a lot of content; case in point, we just returned from Lanai where the Four Seasons opened an all new resort there, absolutely beautiful. So, I taped pretty much a generic interview that I can use in the business show, in the wine show, in the boomer show, and we can offer that as a podcast as well.

Chris: Wow! With all the advances in technology like podcasting, what's the future of radio?

Brian: Well, there's a lot of concern. It's been that way though since the early to mid 1990's. Back then, when the internet came along, a lot of people said this is the end of radio as we know it. I think radio has survived and in some cases thrived over the past 20 years in spite of itself, because as a business, it really has not engaged on that digital platform to the extent that I think it could or should. It's going to be very interesting to see what happens over the next 10 to 15 and maybe 20 years as the millennials come along and we have kids who want everything on demand. They're not used to commercials. They don't like to hear commercials. It's a totally different world, so I think you're going to see a generational shift now as the kids who are; even teenagers right now; migrate into the workforce and beyond. I think we'll see a lot more opportunity for podcasting, on demand content, and I think that broadcast radio stations will really have to embrace digital. They talk about it. They say they're going to do it, but they really haven't fully implemented that.

Chris: You've got the concept of podcasting. The concept of traditional broadcast radio. Now there's kind of a hybrid with online radio, is there not?

Brian: Yeah. You see that as another outlet and it'll be interesting to see how that plays out over the next few years. There are so many outlets for content right now. It circles back to what we talked about earlier. It has to be engaging. It has to be good. I remember way back in college, my professor at the time, this was before the internet, said back then, "It's not about broadcasting. It's about narrowcasting." That was the term he used and this was pretty insightful back in the late 1980's to be saying that about something that hadn't even happened yet, but that's exactly what happened. People want the content that they specifically are interested in and they can literally tune out everything they don't want. Unless it's major breaking news, people are going to focus on what they're interested in, so that's a huge opportunity obviously, for those of us that focus on boomer content or wine content or business content. We can deliver a very specific level of content and a specific demographic for our audience.

Chris: You know, in marketing we say that you should niche and then niche again.

Brian: Yes.

Chris: Be laser beamed focused on who your audience is.

Brian: Definitely. Yes.

Chris: Well, let me ask this question before we get out of here today Brian. What advice would you give to somebody who is thinking, "You know what? I think I might like to do a radio show?"

Brian: Do your homework and do it right. I think there's so many people out there who are good now. Ten years ago that wasn't the case. Now you have a lot of quality podcasts out there, so first of all, practice. That's the number one thing you can do before you hit the air. There's no rule that says you got to put your first one on the air. Tape as many of them as you can. Listen to them. Let your friends, let people who will give you honest feedback, hear what you're doing because that's the best thing right there, is to get some good honest feedback before you ever put it out there into cyberspace.

I would also say you want to have a ton of content. It's remarkable. We produce eight hours of live radio every week and even with a full-time producer and a full-time scheduler we burn through content. I mean, like you would not believe. So, it's really hard to stay out in front of enough content to fill that hour or two. Now with a podcast, maybe we're talking ten or fifteen minutes but even with that, with the schedules and things that come up, you really need to be scheduled out at least six to eight weeks in advance so you have plenty of content to cushion those inevitable dips in your schedule.

Chris: All right. That's great advice. Brian, thanks for joining us today.

Brian: You bet, Chris. Good to see you.

You can reach Brian at brian@feedback-media.com.

Darren Loken

Darren Loken is President of K&H Printing. Darren helps companies, both big and small, effectively use direct mail for client acquisition. He is one of the top experts in his field.

Chris: Darren, thanks for taking time out of your busy schedule to visit with me today.

Darren: Happy to, Chris. Thank you for having me.

Chris: Darren, we're going to go do a deep dive into direct mail. Before we do that, can you give us a brief background of Darren Loken?

Darren: You bet. Born and raised in Seattle, Chris. I'm one of those guys that went to school for marketing. I ended up working in my field. I've made a career for 25 years in direct mail production, primarily on the print side.

Chris: Darren, in your opinion, is direct mail more effective or less effective than in the past?

Darren: There was a point in time where direct mail was handled more in a manner of spraying and praying, we call it. People would mail to the masses and pray for a 2% response rate. The advent of e-mail marketing forced us as direct marketers to be much more effective with the printed direct mail campaign. Over the years, it's become incredibly effective. Much more so because we had to. We were forced to.

Chris: Let me follow up on that. Overall, what impact has online had on direct mail?

Darren: Initially, online without question was a disruptive technology to traditional direct mail programs. Over time, what we've seen is that e-mail has become the modern day spam. People are turning back to traditional direct mail. As mentioned before, they're doing their direct mail much more effectively, because we've had to. We're focusing on campaigns that are data driven, much more relevant for the recipient. Much more effective, where we try to achieve double digit response rates in every campaign that we produce today.

Chris: Which would be awesome, obviously, to get a double-digit response. I want to go back to something you said on the 2%. My experience is so many people who do direct mail focus on the 2%, versus the amount of revenue they generate from their investment. Do you think they're looking at the wrong end of the problem there?

Darren: Everything for direct mail today is about getting return on your investment. You need to focus on a campaign that is really driving towards, as I mentioned earlier, data driven, and offers that are relevant to the recipient. Historically, when we were focusing on the 2%, it was mailing to the masses, and it was all about how pretty the mail piece looked. Prettiness, or creativity, is really the least important part of the mail piece. It's a tried and true statistic that the creative part of the mail piece is accountable for about 20% of the response rate. The data, or list, is 40% of the success. The offer is another 40%. If you focus on your offer and you focus on your data, and when I'm talking about data, we used to only focus on demographics or geographics. Demographics are statistical information like age, height, sex and income. But today, we focus on the psychographics, which are interests, likes, and hobbies. If you are targeting an audience and you are promoting and even sharing imagery, offers, and messages that are relevant to the recipient, you are going to drive up your response rates significantly.

Chris: It was very interesting. You mentioned offers. I see so many people do direct mail and there is no offer or no call-to-action. It's kind of, as you said before, kind of just praying that something happens.

Darren: Yeah, people love to talk about themselves, and they think that is what's most important to the recipient, how great we are, how fabulous we are, we're the biggest, the best, the fastest. That's not what's important. What's important, is what does the recipient want to receive? The offer has got to be something that's going to give them a call to action, that is compelling, and again, I keep using this word, relevant. It's all about relevance.

Chris: Could you give us maybe a couple examples of what an offer and/or a call-to-action might be in a direct mail campaign?

Darren: A very successful direct mail campaign, which had an offer that was relevant to the recipient, was when Target stores decided that they were going to get in to the wedding registry business. They actually knew by the bride and groom's registry what items people actually bought them. So, they knew exactly what the people received, and more importantly, they knew what they didn't receive. Two weeks after the wedding, they produced a small catalogue that was personalized to the bride and groom with only the items that were on their wedding registry list, and in fact would offer them discounts on some of the items that they knew weren't purchased. They needed a table set of 8 and they knew they only received 4. They would give them a modest discount. So, it was very relevant, it's personalized, the offer is exactly what this bride and groom wanted. This campaign got a 100% response rate. It's the only 100% response rate campaign I've ever heard of in my life. That is the best example I can think of as something that's got an offer that is timely and is important to the recipient. When you transport that into your business and think about, "what is it that we have that is going to be timely and important and relevant to my recipient?

Chris: What a great example. Also, one of the things obviously, they had the data to be able to send it to the right people.

Darren: Exactly.

Chris: All the things you talked about earlier were obviously evident in that particular direct mail campaign.

Darren: Data, personalized, relevant, imagery, everything. It was an absolutely beautiful campaign.

Chris: Give us another example of a successful campaign.

Darren: Another example, is that we do work for an organization that tries to match up children in third world countries for a sponsorship by donors here in the United States. They've always focused on tugging at your heartstrings. These folks decided that the imagery of the child, and some personal information about the child, was what was most relevant to the recipients of these targets for their campaigns. They would produce a piece that had an image and details about the child and when you opened up this particular mail package, it would launch a miniature video of that child that tied to the mail piece.

These folks are getting 25% plus response rates based on this relevant and personal emotive direct mail campaign.

Chris: People are automatically thinking, "Oh my goodness, that would be so expensive, it wouldn't make sense in my business." But, I'm guessing the return this organization is getting far exceeds any amount that they're spending.

Darren: It's unbelievable.

Chris: It really is amazing. I'm going to go back to something you said regarding the data. Tell us a little bit about how easy it is to get really detailed data, both from demographics and combine it with psychographics.

Darren: When you look at the databases that are possible, the best database is always your own. What do you know about what your customers or prospective customers have been doing? Combining your own database with other sources of data, up to and including subscription databases, which you know based on the subscription to a particular magazine. And by the way, in the United States, you can rent the list from over 40,000 different subscription magazines. If you're trying to sell something that's going to appeal to somebody who likes sports, or marine activities, canoeing, kayaking, golfing, or lacrosse, you can actually get data for any one of those activities and supplement them with your own database.

Chris: That's just awesome. It really is remarkable how specific we can get that list down to, correct?

Darren: Absolutely.

Chris: Obviously Darren, companies are using direct mail to get responses. Typically what they're using them for is prospecting. Those salespeople will get responses and then I'm guessing they're using it schedule appointments. Do you have any examples of companies that have had success that way?

Darren: Some of our customers, home improvement organizations, will mail to neighborhoods that fit their profile for age of home and that have income propensity that they might be good candidates to spend money for improving their home energy efficiency. They'll set appointments, literally, from the direct mail campaigns with their sales force to go into the home and provide a home energy audit for free. That opens the door to a myriad of potential sales opportunities, whether it be windows, air conditioning, heating and insulation.

Chris: Okay, so we have a great demographics data. We have a great offer which leads to somebody wanting a free energy audit, which leads to an appointment, which eventually leads to a sale.

Darren: Absolutely.

Chris: That's the way direct mail generates sales for organizations. We're combining two things here, correct? There's a free offer, in this case a home energy audit, where people are thinking, "Wow, it's free." Obviously, the organization is using it as the foot the door to eventually make a sale. More importantly, they're in there, they're establishing credibility by going through the energy audit, which leads, many times, to the sale.

Darren: Exactly.

Chris: It's really interesting. I was talking to somebody on your sales team. They were telling me that with one of your customers, you actually had to stop mailing, because the first couple of mailings were so successful, their sales people couldn't keep up with the activity.

Darren: Yeah, it sounds odd doesn't it? That can happen. That's important in your planning process. If you achieve too great a response and you can't respond to them, you're doing more damage, doing more harm than good.

Chris: Okay, so those are a couple of examples of B-to-C. What's happening in the B-to-B market when it comes to direct mail?

Darren: We're seeing two major trends in B-to-B direct mail marketing. The first of which is where the direct mail is purposed entirely to drive traffic online, whether it's providing a personalized URL, or our slang for that in our trade is called a PURL. This is where the recipient will enter in their own URL and it will put them on a landing page that's personalized and relevant to the recipient. You're tying the tactile nature of a printed, direct mail piece with an online personalized message, and, by the way unbelievable trackability. The other opportunities that people are utilizing are what are called quick response codes, or QR codes. This is a two-dimensional barcode where, when scanned with your mobile device, will launch a video to provide an opportunity for a presentation, or more information for the company and its offer. The other thing that we're seeing much more of is a transition from traditional self-mailers or envelope mailers or letters, to what we refer to as dimensional mailers. This is where people are literally spending a little bit more in the direct mail package that may include items that are compelling, or will have staying power and get the door open. We refer to them often times as bunker busters. Busting the door open for the sales force, or for an opportunity in the B-to-B application. Spending more money, investing in dimensional mailers, and packages with maybe some gifts, or something a little more substantive than just your traditional sending out a postcard or self-mailer, and hoping that the business professional is going to take a look at it.

Chris: You had an example of that with your company, where you sent something special to your current clients, just as a token of appreciation.

Darren: Customer appreciation is clearly something that we believe in, both for promoting it to our customers, but utilizing for our company. We tend to time our customer appreciation events around non-traditional holidays. For example, recently we had a Mardi Gras Fat Tuesday promotion, where we literally sent King Cakes to our top customers, as an appreciation gift. And the thing that we like most about it is, it's something that's shared throughout the organization. It's just not one person getting it. That cake lands, and the entire office or organization is huddled around it in the lunchroom with our name all over it.

Chris: That's awesome. From what I understand, it was an overwhelming success, correct?

Darren: Unbelievable. And, it was unique.

Chris: Darren, before we leave the B-to-B discussion, I think it's very, very important that so often, companies think offline *or* online. In reality, is it fair to say that most companies should do both?

Darren: We believe so. It's not just because we're driving printed direct mail volume, but marrying the two is the best of both worlds. As I mentioned earlier, if you're doing only e-mail marketing, or only direct mail marketing, or only online marketing, you're missing the most effective mediums. It's about using all the mediums from our perspective. Our customers have much greater success when they're doing multi-media campaigns, including direct mail, and helping drive traffic to their stores, drive traffic to their websites, or create opportunities for their sales force.

Chris: I think what I'd like the readers to leave with is, "Hey look, you probably should be using online, and you should be using offline, and by the way, why not use offline to drive people online?" It really tends to be, as you said, a big part of the trend.

Darren: Without question.

Chris: Before we get out of here today Darren, what would be maybe the final pieces of advice you would give to anybody who is thinking, "You know what, I want to implement direct mail in my marketing and prospecting efforts"?

Darren: First of all, it's all about the planning. Direct mail is all about ROI. To achieve the ROI, you have to be able to measure it. That's one of the things we love about direct mail. It's tactile, it's measurable. We know what the response is. We know whether or not we're making money. Repeating some of what I said earlier, it's got to be personalized. It's got to be relevant to the recipient. You've got to take into consideration a strong offer that's going to be accountable for 40% of your response. Your data, which is another 40%, and how perfect is that for your audience. Then creative, although important, is the least important piece in all that. People again focus way too much on how pretty the piece looks, rather we want effective direct mail. We want double-digit response rates, day in, day out, and that's all achieved by personalization, the relevance, the planning, the psychographics, the offer and the data.

Chris: I hope the readers take advantage of the types of services that are out there, because I can't imagine how much success they're going to have if they get double-digit response to their direct mail.

Darren: Absolutely.

Chris: Darren, thanks for your time today.

Darren: You bet, my pleasure.

Darren's website is www.khprint.com

Michael Alf

After a global corporate career, Michael Alf decided to start his own business, offering services in the digital transformation space. Michael is the author of multiple, #1 Best Selling books, one of which is *The Virtual Summit Formula: How your virtual summit can attract thousands of participants, grow your email list, and boost your business.*

Michael works with entrepreneurs and companies to create virtual summits that attract hundreds and thousands of participants, grow and elevate their business and create significant exposure in the marketplace.

Originally from Germany, Michael is currently living the dream with his family in Melbourne, Australia.

Chris: Michael, I really want to thank you for taking time out of your busy schedule to meet with me today.

Michael: Chris, it's a great pleasure to be here. Thank you very much for the invite.

Chris: All the way from Melbourne, Australia and I know we're going to talk about virtual summits in depth, but before we do that, Michael, can you give us just a brief background of Michael Alf?

Michael: Absolutely, Chris. It's my pleasure. As you can hear, I'm not really Australian, though I live in Melbourne, Australia now. I'm German. Seven years ago, I had the opportunity with my family to move from Germany to Australia, to Melbourne, and we took that opportunity. It was with a company I was working with, one of the world's largest IT companies. It has been an interesting journey since then, since we landed here in Australia with the family. We just loved it. From there, after a while, after a couple of years actually, I started my own entrepreneur journey and that's what I'm doing now, passionately. I believe in entrepreneurship. It's really great to be here, but also then connecting with other people around the globe, like yourself.

Chris: Yeah, it was a real honor to meet you a little over a year ago. We actually met in San Diego.

Michael: Yes, in San Diego.

Chris: Michael, you left the corporate world, you became an entrepreneur. Tell us about your current business model.

Michael: Yeah, so we have two main services right now which we're offering, which helps basically people to explore online and position themselves in the marketplace. Those are books, so I help people actually to publish books and become an international best-selling author. We have fixed packages where I work with individuals, business people, and others who want to use it as a positioning tool. That's one.

The other one is what we're talking about here, virtual summits. Again, the business model there is evolving from a complete basically done for you package, which we're now offering. I'm also doing still some consulting and interim management work right now for a software company, where I'm basically helping here in Australia to run the business. That's kind of my current model.

Chris: When you talk about virtual summits and you thought about doing those, was it a bolt of lightning that hit you or did the idea of doing virtual summits come to you gradually?

Michael: That's an excellent question, Chris. It goes back to one of these conferences. One of the things I figured out quickly, is that I need to learn from the best. You always need to watch out who's in the market and who's doing new and innovative things, and how do you actually get in touch? I spend a lot of time and money on conferences, learning from people. I think it became a combination of things, but there was one conference in San Diego in 2014 where somebody presented actually that concept of a summit. We thought that's really great. That sounds really exciting, so we decided to basically test that and run our own first virtual summit. That was exactly a year ago in March 2015. It was a huge success. It was for my wife's business. This was the foundation. I then created the book *The Virtual Summit Formula* really to put that into practice what I'm preaching and helping other people, obviously, but also putting that into a process, into a formula.

Chris: Was it doing your wife's virtual summit that was really the tipping point to say, "Okay, this is going to be a huge part of my business"?

Michael: Yeah, absolutely. I would say so. We clearly saw the potential. We saw what you can do with it in terms of list building, in terms of creating money, in terms of connecting. I said, "We have to do that." There is so much potential out there, and since then, I have so many ideas where this can add value to various organizations, businesses, small, medium, large. I think there's a huge opportunity there.

Chris: Now, Michael, I know a little bit about the back story to that summit you're referring to, but maybe could you give us some of the highlights in terms of the business success that resulted as a result of that summit?

Michael: Yeah, absolutely. That first summit, we created, keep in mind, that is Australian numbers. Australia is only a fraction of the population United States. That first summit, I created 3500 participants. When you do the math, so we are around 20 million, you are 320 million, so you can multiply that by almost 20 to get an idea. Adding 3500 people to your list in only a few weeks, I assume, is attractive for every single business. Even better, we created actually 350 paying clients out of it. You basically, within a few weeks, you have 350 people who actually pull out their credit card and give you money. I think that was really one of the biggest benefits out of it in terms of commercialism. We've seen similar results after that as well.

Chris: That's a great story. What's the process that you go through to create and host a virtual summit?

Michael: It's a multi-step approach and I talk in detail and really break that down in the book, _**The Virtual Summit Formula.**_ Basically a lot is in the preparation phase. That phase is really, really critical where you think about your target market, your avatar or your ideal customer you want to attract to the summit, and what problem you're going to solve with the virtual summit. I think that's one of the key findings out of all the summits we're now doing, that this is really, really important to make attractive and interesting. Then, you need to think about the speakers. We have the concept of anchor speaker, which is someone very popular and who pulls in not only the audience, but also other speakers. That all is in the preparation phase, which is the first phase.

Then it's the setup phase. Obviously, there's a lot of technology involved. There are systems which need to play together from a front end system which is capturing leads, a summit area, a video platform, a payment platform, so we have multiple systems which play together. You set everything up, and then you actually drive traffic to it and you test that.

Then, you have the execution phase, which is quite intense because everything needs to run smoothly. You need to be aware of what's happening because it's an online event. It's a different environment than a typical physical summit.

Then the last phase, is what do you do now after the summit? How do you grow? How do you utilize what you've built and what you've put together?

Chris: You had mentioned payment processing. A summit doesn't have to be a paid summit, correct?

Michael: That is very true, yes, Chris. You can offer free summits, and as a matter of fact, most of our summits are free initially, but then we basically offer the recordings in a bonus package afterwards, and a certain percentage of people are buying that. You don't have to do that. You can do, if you like, for example, a not-for-profit summit. You make it completely free.

Chris: If I am a participant, if you will, I'm viewing the virtual summit, one of the beauties, as I understand it, is I can pick and choose which of the presentations or which of the speakers that I want to listen to or view, correct?

Michael: Absolutely. Yeah, that is one of the big

advantages. When you think about it, you go to a typical conference. So you fly there and you need accommodations, and then typically you sit there and listen through everything, and you might do other things on your computer or whatever. Not everything is the same value. Here, you have much more flexibility. You can say, "I'll pick, out of 12 speakers over 3 days, I like these 5 the most, so I'll listen into those." Then, when there's an offer of summit package, the recordings, now you can actually go back afterwards and listen to them again, which is very difficult when you do that in a physical environment.

Chris: It really is something that I've thought about when I read your book. Like you, I attend lots of conferences, lots of summits live, if you will, and the amount of time, effort, and money that goes into that, although I always get value out of it, there's a lot of what I call dead time.

Michael: Yeah, absolutely. When I think here from Australia and you have to travel, for example, to the United States, obviously you have really great experts in this field of marketing, internet marketing, sales and all that, but there's a lot of travel and cost involved.

Chris: Well, let me ask you this, what's been the biggest surprises, good or bad, about doing virtual summits?

Michael: On the positive, I think one point I would like to bring up is the connection you are getting with other speakers. I've seen amazing examples where we ran a summit and we had global speakers and when they got together and they connected. I can see now how much business is coming out of that amongst the speakers. Even though it's virtual, they're still connecting. We have these live sessions via Blab or others, where they actually sit together and we discuss and we have fun, and that opportunity for the host, especially when you start out, to connect with celebrities in your niche, in your market, that is probably one of the most positive surprises.

On a flip side, on the negative side, there's lots of learnings in every single summit. Because the concept is still relatively new, but there are things like, do you get enough traffic? Do you get enough people to sign in? Then, even more so, how do you actually engage them and bring people back so that they actually listen to the content you are providing? This is where you can have some disappointments, and you see, especially when you do a longer summit, you see a significant drop off. It's almost like a physical summit, where typically on a Sunday, if it's a Friday, Saturday, Sunday meeting, so from Sunday noon on, people actually leaving, not showing up anymore, and even when the highlight speaker is there on Sunday afternoon, you still have a drop off. That's one of the things we see in virtual summits as well.

Chris: Do you find that a certain length of a summit has been working better than another, i.e. a one or two day versus a three or four day or longer?

Michael: Yeah, it's a very good question and we test around. I find, at the moment, I would keep them shorter rather than longer. Shorter, I mean around three days max, because then it is actually an event, and it's not an on-going thing which can be over two weeks. One of our first summits was held over a two week period. It's very, very intense on the organizer side, on the participant side, and it becomes incredibly overwhelming. Also, the participants said, "well, it's just too much content, too many speakers, so I can't be bothered to listen anymore." That's the risk you're running. If it's short and sharp and high quality, it's more doable and more manageable for the participants.

Chris: Michael, I've seen, on the virtual summit, three different things. I'm sure that there're more, but I'm just going to ask you a question based upon what I've seen. I've seen a presenter do what I call a talking PowerPoint, I've seen them do a face to camera, where they're talking directly to the camera, kind of in a very intimate setting, and then I've seen them actually be on a stage making a presentation or in front of a room. What's your advice, or is there a best way to get the message across on a virtual summit?

Michael: Yeah, again, you're right. There's different

models. There's even more models. One of the probably most dominant models, you mentioned the PowerPoint talk, that's one. The other one is actually an interview. One of the other summits we did, the majority of the presentations were actually interviews with experts, and that has some beauty because actually you connect and it's more engaging and entertaining for the participants, because that is really, really important. I think what is difficult is if you have boring PowerPoint presentations. We all know how it is to sit for an hour in front of a PowerPoint presentation. You want to have this interaction and that excitement and this entertainment effect. That's why I believe standing in front of a camera can actually be really something very positive and working with a whiteboard, like Brendon Buchard. He does that brilliantly. Something like that is very powerful.

The other one is interviews. Interviews can be Skype interviews, but what also worked very well is actually live interviews. There is a little bit more effort on the host side, but you actually see people and you record the interviews live which, again, gives it different flair. For example, cooking demonstrations is a nice one. That's what we did a couple of times. You have that mix, but what is key is really how to make it exciting, interesting, and inviting.

Chris: Those are some great points. A comment I want to make, you said earlier about getting the speakers together, because one of the things I know that some naysayers are going to be thinking or saying is, "Well, you can't establish relationships on a virtual summit." But you already said that in the pre-work, in having all the speakers together on a particular platform, be it Blab or be it a conference call, or a webinar, or Skype, or whatever, they're actually developing and deepening relationships, even though it is "virtual".

Michael: Yes, absolutely. Look, I'm the first to admit, and I think I even write that on the back of my book, saying, I'm not against physical summits, and they will have their place. They are more important than ever before, because of the speed of change and things we need to learn and want to learn. The point is, you have so much new stuff coming in, so we need new models to actually communicate and distribute information and connect people. I see two things. One is, it's clearly more difficult for the participants to connect, but again, when you think about a specific Facebook group and things like that, there are things you can do. I'd say that is less powerful than on a physical summit, but there's one downside. You can't have a beer with another participant.

Chris: Being from Australia, you got to have your beer, right?

Michael: Yes, absolutely.

Chris: Being a German who lives in Australia, you have to have beer.

Michael: Both German and Australian, that's so true, Chris. On the speaker side, and this is really, really important, because a lot of the speakers, obviously, are now partially in the online world, so they are used to connecting online. This is really, really powerful, because you bring them together and either they communicate on a live chat, or even when they are on the same one, they might then connect and reach out and you have new connections and new business opportunities coming out of it.

Chris: Well, Michael, as an entrepreneur, what impact have virtual summits had on your particular business?

Michael: I already spoke about the financial impact we saw from the first summit. I would say, 2015 was the start-up year, so we did 5 virtual summits. Basically, because of that success and the interest in the market, I'm taking that now to the next level. As we speak, I think I have around 10 summits already in the pipeline with more discussions happening, and as a consequence, we're building now a team who can actually run the shows in a very professional, structured way so that you get the right quality level. I see a huge business opportunity there, and I'm excited about this year and the following years.

Chris: What advice would you give to someone who is considering doing a virtual summit?

Michael: Honestly, I think we're just tapping and scratching the surface here. I think it can be relevant for almost every single business, especially when you are in a certain niche. We're working on a summit in the recruiting industry, for example, right now. We're doing one in the business transformation space, in the entrepreneur space, in the health space. I mean, you can tap into almost everything, and you can niche it even further down. It is a great way to, obviously, attract your audience and your customers. I also see the opportunity for larger organizations to actually use that both for their customers. Imagine, Coca-Cola could do a summit, a global summit, virtual summit, and actually bring all their stars, promotion stars together, get access to them virtually, and interact with them and do that in a summit environment. Even that's a B-2-C segment and environment.

You could also bring together, when you run a business, you could do a supplier summit, virtual summit. Let's say you have, I don't know, 100 suppliers for your business, and you can organize a supplier business. You can actually, when you want to position yourself in the marketplace as an expert in a field, let's say software, you could run a summit in this area and even invite competitors to that summit. Obviously, because you are hosting and you're providing, you position yourself in front of a large audience. Hopefully, that gives an idea that there's so much potential and so many opportunities to utilize the concept of the virtual summit.

Chris: I agree wholeheartedly, Michael. One of the things that I've compared it to is podcasting. Right now, podcasting is incredibly popular, and I think virtual summits are the next podcasting. Right now, to your point, people who get in on it early, they have about a 3 to 5 year head start on what will be mainstream in a few years.

Michael: Yes, I agree. I see that potential. What is really exciting is that the variety, how you can utilize and use that. I mean, you can do one about beer brewing, yeah? You can bring all the local brewers from Australia and US and Canada and Germany together and have a fun beer-brewing summit with live demonstrations. I think there's really some exciting opportunities.

Chris: The one downside there is you don't get to taste it if it's virtual.

Michael: I mean, that's something we're working on. One of the ideas, and that's probably looking into the future a little bit, how do you combine online and offline? That's what I want to do, hopefully this year, but definitely next year, how do you combine both elements and components and bring that together in a new way? You have a global summit with local gatherings, supported by the virtual concept, if you like.

Chris: Well, make sure when you send out the mailer for the online virtual summit for beer brewing that you send me an advance copy.

Michael: I will, Chris.

Chris: Well, Michael, you've been very gracious with your time, and I have two questions before I let you go today. Number one, could you tell us again the name of your book that you wrote regarding virtual summits that everybody should pick up?

Michael: Absolutely, Chris. It's *The Virtual Summit Formula*. When you go to Amazon or Google my name, Michael Alf, or Virtual Summit Formula.

Chris: Awesome. Then, secondly, if somebody has some further questions and they want to learn more about either a coaching opportunity in virtual summits or the do it for yourself virtual summits, what's the best way for somebody to get a hold of you?

Michael: E-mail, michael@virtualsummitformula.com. Like the book title, virtualsummitformula.com and Michael as the first name.

Chris: Well, Michael, thanks for taking time out of your busy schedule to visit with us today.

Michael: Thank you, Chris. It was a great pleasure. Have a wonderful day.

I interviewed each one of these experts in an effort to find out their "secret sauce." Hopefully, you will use some of these as you are creating your recipe for success.

CONCLUSION

If you have made it all the way through this book, you are probably asking yourself, "does this really work?" After all, how many authors have written books based on a theory, not experience?

Well, let me briefly tell you my story.

A little over three years before this book was written, I had been working with an organization doing Sales Training and Sales Coaching. I had been with the company for 10 years. I had no reason to think that I would not be there for another 10 years. Then, literally, overnight, everything changed. I was told that my services were no longer needed. Unfortunately for me, that company owned all of the clients I was working with. So, in an instant my world was rocked.

While the income went away, the bills did not. The bills for the mortgage, tuitions for private colleges and payment on the vacation home still had to be paid. I had no desire to return to the corporate world, so I had to find clients real fast. I wish I could tell you that I am so smart that I deliberately and strategically built my new company based on Publishing, Speaking and Referrals. But as it turns out, that is exactly what I did. No cold calling, and no advertising, either online or offline.

The results? In my first year, I exceeded the prior year's income I had with the organization I just left. In my second year, I made more money than I ever have in my life. In my third year, I exceeded that second year's income.

Now, I tell you this not to brag, because I do not think that I am all that special. There are many readers of this book

51088333R00106

Made in the USA
Lexington, KY
11 April 2016